The Steward

A Biblical Symbol Come Of Age

The Steward

A Biblical Symbol Come Of Age

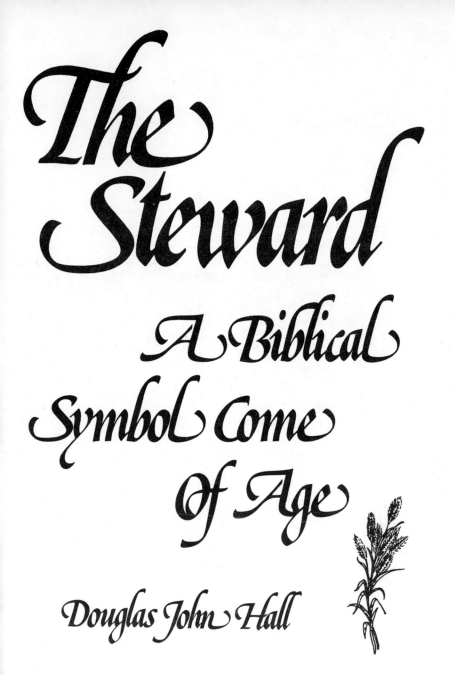

Douglas John Hall

Friendship Press * New York

for

Commission on Stewardship

National Council of the Churches of Christ in the U.S.A.

LIBRARY OF CHRISTIAN STEWARDSHIP

Handbook of Stewardship Procedures
  T. K. Thompson

Stewardship in Mission
  Winburn T. Thomas

The Christian Meaning of Money
  Otto A. Piper

Stewardship Illustrations
  T. K. Thompson

Why People Give
  Martin E. Carlson

Punctured Preconceptions
  Douglas W. Johnson and
  George W. Cornell

The Steward: A Biblical Symbol Come of Age
  Douglas John Hall

ISBN 0-377-00133-3

© 1982 Commission on Stewardship
            National Council of Churches

            2nd Printing 1983

Dedicated to

Christopher Levan
Don Matheson
Thomas Nordberg
Bernhard Stempel
Brian Thorpe

*and others of their generation
who are being the stewards I
have written about here.*

"... symbols cannot be invented.
Like living beings, they grow and
they die. They grow when the situation
is ripe for them. ..."

—Paul Tillich

CONTENTS

PREFACE

In 1978 I was invited to speak on the subject of Stewardship and Mission at the annual meeting of the Commission on Stewardship of the National Council of the Churches of Christ in the U.S.A. I do not know why this invitation came to me. Certainly I was no expert on stewardship. But as I thought about the subject, certain disconcerting ideas began to occur to me, like Kierkegaard's "thoughts that wound from behind." What emerged from this struggle either interested or astonished or angered or puzzled the Commission, apparently, because I was asked to return in 1979; and, as if they had not already heard more than enough, the Commission invited me to come back a third time and fourth time in 1980 and 1981.

All that homework on the subject of stewardship made me realize that we Christians have been carrying about with us a highly provocative and even revolutionary symbol—whose power we have unfortunately muffled in ecclesiastical wrappings. While the churches trudge along with this ancient metaphor, rather embarrassed by its association with money and properties, the contemporary world of environmentalists and peace marchers and others has been discovering its radical potential. It seemed to me that its time had come, that we might redeem it for Christian use too!

What encouraged me more than anything was that the members of the Commission seemed to think so too. In spite of (no, *because of*) the fact that they were, many of them, people in our various denominations who had the unenviable job of keeping the Ark of Church afloat, they *were* as unhappy as I *became* about the truncation of the symbol. They were perfectly well aware of the fact that starting by asking for money, time, and talents is putting the cart before the horse. Before we can depend on that kind of support from our people, we must show that *being* stewards in and of the world is somehow a vital way of conceiving our whole Christian and human vocation.

This study grew out of my homework for the lectures for the Commission, as well as a booklet that I was asked to prepare for "Church World Development and Relief," published and distributed by five Canadian denominations under the title *This World Must Not Be Abandoned! Stewardship: Its Worldly Meaning*. I have incorporated materials both from this booklet and from my lectures for the Commission in the text of the present study, though in revised form. The study has also been influenced by many conversations in North America and Europe, with pastors, theologians, officers of the World Council of Churches, students, and countless others.

I owe special thanks therefore to a host of persons for stimulating these thoughts and proposals. But I am especially indebted to Dr. Nordan Murphy, Assistant General Secretary of the National Council of Churches for Stewardship, who has been wonderfully supportive throughout these years of my struggle to understand this theme; and to Dr. M. Jewitt Parr and the Reverend Walton H. Tonge of my own church, The United Church of Canada, who have published earlier papers and the aforementioned booklet.

I am of course grateful as well to the Ecumenical Center for Stewardship Studies in Evanston for commissioning me to undertake this study.

—*Douglas John Hall*

Provence, France
Ash Wednesday, 1982

INTRODUCTION

1 Theological Depths in an Ecclesiastical Practice?

North American Christianity is not noted for its theological depth. Ours has been a practical faith, more concerned for the ethical side of the Christian life than for the subtleties of theological investigation or doctrinal distinctions. With a few exceptions, theological trends have been set for us by European thinkers and schools; and our appropriation of the successive waves of theology emanating from the European Mother- and Fatherlands has involved, usually, a notorious simplification and sloganization of their complexities.

This theological innocency is rightly decried by many sensitive North American Christians today. There is a growing recognition amongst us that ethics always presuppose a foundation in one's understanding of reality, that "the Imperative" will not stand by itself but assumes an articulated "Indicative." A faith that is not equipped to express the theological principles upon which its moral values and its practical goals are based is a house without foundations. It may stand while there are no serious assaults upon it; but with the winds of doubt and the storms of social unrest, such a faith must either get foundations or fall to the ground. Dependency upon the foundations laid for other houses (for the European church, for example) will not suffice. Given the realities of religious pluralism and secular skepticism, North American Christianity today finds itself compelled to develop a theological rationale for its pragmatically-oriented faith, and that reason must grow out of its own experience, suffering, and hope.[1]

Paradoxically however there are points where the very practicality of Christianity on this continent has helped it to retain contact with aspects of the faith lost to the more theoretically sophisticated provinces of Christendom. It behooves those who search today for contextual theological expressions of Christianity in North America to pay particular attention to such points. In any case, the pragmatic character of our Christianity could be dismissed as theologically uninteresting or merely naive only by persons who had never really heard that "by their fruits you shall know them"! Besides, there are perhaps hidden depths of potential theological importance in *some* of the practices that inform everyday life in North

American churches. Theological praxis, about which we shall speak more fully presently, must mean reflecting upon these practices with sufficient imagination to wrest from them their deeper meaning, and then permitting the new depth of understanding to inform our actions.

Of the practices in question, none is more provocative than stewardship. Stewardship is one of the givens of North American church life. Every denomination has its division or department of stewardship. Every congregation contains organizational structures to attend to "the stewardship question." The term stewardship, at least in Portestant circles, is familiar to every parishoner— for some altogether too familiar!

Anyone acquainted with European Christianity will realize that this constitutes a *marked* distinction from the churches of our parental culture. The concept of stewardship is largely unheard of in Europe. Even ministers and professional theologians are perplexed by this concept that, in our ecclesiastical setting, is understood immediately by ordinary churchgoers, as well as by many who have long since given up going to church. Though the term has been (rather recently) translated into European language equivalents, it remains a foreign *idea*. The average German layperson, for example, is wholly baffled by the word *Haushalterschaft*[2], so that German scholars and administrators who have become interested in the subject very often employ the English word 'stewardship' in the attempt to introduce the concept to their contemporaries.[3]

The retention in North American church life of an important biblical concept like stewardship does not of course mean that Christians on our continent have been more faithful to their origins than have other Christians in Europe and elsewhere. It is quite simply a consequence of the necessities that were laid upon us by historical providence. Unlike the European parent churches (not all of them, but the most prominent ones), the churches in North America have had to fend for themselves. We have not been altogether "disestablished," of course; for the structure of our societies both in the United States and Canada have favored Christianity from the outset. Not only has the church on this continent been able throughout most of its history to count on being received as "the conscience of society," but it has also enjoyed material benefits such as the exclusion of church properties from taxation. Still, by comparison with European forms of Christian establishment, the churches in North America have been independent, separate, and voluntary organizations whose members have themselves been directly responsible for their maintenance. With few exceptions, therefore, Christian bodies had to develop structures and programs that encouraged the support of their membership and facilitated their . . . stewardship! Not virtue, then, but necessity has been the mother of this invention—as in so many of humanity's

2

nobler achievements. The stewardship idea has been perpetuated in our historical experience because it had to be.

2 An Idea Whose Time Has Come

But taking the biblical view of history as normative (consider the Joseph narrative for instance), one could suppose that what people experience as necessity not infrequently turns out to be providential. Their relative disestablishment in the New World context caused the Christian denominations of this continent to pay attention to what is, after all, a rather prominent biblical metaphor of the life and vocation of the *koinonia*. During the past century or so, the disestablishment ("humiliation") of the church has become an ever more visible phenomenon in Western societies—dramatically so in those societies that have been taken over by ideologies hostile to Christianity and religion; less conspicuously, but perhaps all the more effectively, in the affluent societies of the First World. Even Western European churches whose economic and legal position vis à vis the State seems altogether secure face a highly uncertain future. In West Germany, the state-collected church tax ensures an exceptionally prosperous church—to the extent that the World Council of Churches budget relies upon West German Protestantism to the tune of 30 percent.[4] But West German churches are sparsely attended, and nothing but convention and inconvenience stands between the continuation of this form of establishment and the advent of a new and (to many) threatening ecclesiastical proverty. Critical voices within the West German church even suggest that the church itself ought to take initiative in cutting the apron strings with the official culture. But this would of course thrust congregations into a degree of self-reliance for which they are on the whole ill prepared. The experience of several centuries of stewardship practice *could*, if North American Christians became more reflective about their meaning, be of enormous help to Christians the world over facing the necessity of making the difficult transition from established to non- or disestablished forms of the church. The church on this continent could turn out to have been a kind of pilot project in post-Constantinian Christianity, or at least a stage on the way.

Such a prospect has not been lost on far-sighted churchmen/women in other settings. Already in the early 1950s the well-known German theologian and churchman Bishop Hanns Lilje drew attention to the importance of this North American contribution to ecumenical thought and practice:

> "To know that with all that we are and all that we have we are God's stewards is the answer to a particularly deep yearning of the time in which we live, namely, the yearning for a *vita nova*, a complete re-

newal of our life. Here the insights of our American brethren in the faith have, in the perspective of church history, something like the same significance as the lessons which the German Lutheran Reformation has taught us about justification by grace, or the Communion of the Brethren about the unity of God's children."[5]

To compare the significance of the stewardship idea worked out in North American ecclesiastical experience with the Reformation's teaching on justification seems extravagant—until two things are realized, one about the church, the other about the world. As a survivor of Hitler's Germany, Bishop Lilje knew well enough that the church had to move out into a new realm of freedom from the dominant culture if it were ever to make good its calling to be a prophetic voice in God's world. Such freedom could not be had by a church that continued to rely upon established power for its rudimentary support. Stewardship in the North American experience is significant, therefore, not merely as a managerial technique for funding the church's life and work, but as a dimension of a new understanding of the church as such. What North American Christians have to contribute has, for Lilje, a high significance because stewardship practice is in effect the most visible side of a whole *alternative image of the church*.

But the context of the quotation we have cited indicates that Bishop Lilje also sensed the importance of stewardship as a way of thinking and being beyond the confines of the church itself. He writes with the knowledge of a thoughtful European at the end of a time of devastation and nihilism; and as such a one he knows, as did many of his contemporaries, that nothing but a new appreciation for the worth and wonder of life could deliver Western humanity from its self-destructive impulses. Just as the Lutheran vision of a justifying "grace through faith" enabled people in an age of anxiety over "eternal guilt and condemnation" (Tillich) to find the courage to go on, so, Lilje is affirming, the sense of being stewards of earth and all life could provide a generation of world-weary and apathetic 'survivors' with some feeling of *purpose*.

In the 30 years that have elapsed since Lilje's provocative statement was written, his assumptions both about the church and the world have been confirmed by events. The church has almost everywhere found itself being edged out of the center of the Establishment—though many militant Christians still labor hard to reinstate it! As for the world, we know by now that the state of chaos and panic that broke out in two World Wars during the first half of this century, with its accompanying moods of violence on the one hand and apathy on the other, cannot be regarded as unusual. War, hot and cold, has been the hallmark of this whole century, which was supposed to have been "The Christian Century."[6] Beyond that, we are conscious of living under the shadow of a future holocaust

4

that could put an end to all that our foundational traditions meant by 'civilization.' This "future shock" has produced, predictably enough, exaggerated forms of withdrawal from public life and responsibility. In the still affluent world of the North Atlantic nations, human beings seek comfort in the narcissistic cultivation of the private life, leaving the future to forces that are as indifferent to the quality of life as they are "leaderless" (Martin Buber). In short, the times are calling for stewards of Earth in a way that has never been so true in human experience heretofore.

What is so encouraging and at the same time so humbling is that the articulation of this call for the stewarding of the world is being voiced more insistently and, often, more imaginatively today by secular humanists, scientists, and others than by Christians as such. In recent years, Christianity has come under a new kind of criticism—one that could hardly have been anticipated prior to World War II. As we shall remind our readers in the following discussions, many of the most sensitive critics of Western civilization today accuse the Hebraic-Christian tradition of having laid the theoretical-spiritual foundations for a society that has pursued *mastery* of Earth to the point of ruination. Unlike the "scientific" critics of religion who used to accuse Christians of holding backward concepts of the universe and thus retarding human Progress, the new critics accuse the biblical tradition of putting it into the heads of Western peoples that they were in charge of the natural world ("Have dominion!") and might do as they pleased to ensure human advancement. More of that later. The point at the moment is that these same critics of an imperialist Christendom, when they cast about for any *good* that might have come out of Nazareth, point with uncanny unanimity to the concept of stewardship. Here, they say, is an image of humanity, that, if it were pursued with some imagination, could offset the bad effects of a religion that made too much of humankind's superiority to the natural world.

In sum, then, the stewardship tradition, which is rooted in biblical religion and has of necessity been retained in the experience of North American Christianity, has come of age. It is a mode of being sorely needed by an ecumenical church that (Deo gratia!) can no longer count upon being the darling of power. It is even more badly needed by a world that has fallen into the clutches of mindless and inherently destructive forces. Logically, one could suppose that Christian churches with several centuries of practical experience in stewardship would, under these circumstances, find themselves in a position of something like expertise. But in fact we do not and cannot feel such confidence in ourselves. Our practice of stewardship has not, after all, given us the insight that we need to make the kind of contribution that Lilje and others anticipate from us. What stands in the way of it?

5

3 The Truncation of the Concept

Just here it is necessary to be quite honest with ourselves. It is true that the stewardship dimension has been retained in our 'New World' Christianity. But it is equally true that it has been retained in a form that scarcely lends itself to the larger meaning and usage that our historical moment calls for. What we have by way of stewardship is in fact a greatly reduced version of the biblical concept.

It would perhaps be kinder to say that it is a purely *functional* appropriation of the term. That is, for the majority of churchgoers stewardship signifies a way of thinking about (one could almost say of rationalizing!) the acquisition and management of ecclesiastical monies and properties. Stewardship as *means*. One tries to inculcate a sense of stewardship in congregations *so that* the church might get on with its "real" work. The *end* in relation to which stewardship is a means is something spiritual and noble. Often, as a way of contrasting it with stewardship, this end is designated the church's "mission." Stewardship must be cultivated in order to facilitate the mission. It is the material means by which the spiritual end is achieved.

This typical justification for stewardship in the churches, while it can made to seem high minded, has in fact ensured that stewardship can only with difficulty be raised to the level of an holistic metaphor for Christian and human life. So thoroughly associated is the term with church management and finances; so demeaned is it by the implicitly unfavorable comparison with the spiritual mission for which it is only the means, that it will require a great deal of critical thought and work to bring the stewardship metaphor to the prominence its biblical background warrants and the times call for. If, as we have hinted above, the world is today more apt than the church to find the idea of the steward provocative, it is largely, I suspect, because in the churches the metaphor has been relegated to a strictly functional and instrumental status.

The extent to which the steward metaphor has *suffered* from our stewardship practices is reflected in the fact (I alluded to it in passing earlier) that for many churchgoers, including clergy, the term has a decidedly distasteful connotation. It at once conjures up the horrors of every-person visitations, building projects, financial campaigns, and the seemingly incessant harping of the churches for more money. Ministers cringe at the mention of Stewardship Sundays: must they really lower themselves to the status of fundraiser once more? Must they again play the role of a Tetzel?[7]

The demeaning of stewardship is even built into the organizational structures of the churches. The practice of dividing the work of the congregation into matters handled by the Session or Elders (spiritual items) and, on the other hand, by the Board of Stewards (material matters) has happily been abandoned in favor of unified boards of management in many denominations. Yet the thinking that expressed itself in such divisions has by no means disappeared. Few of us would say so openly, but there is a kind of tacit understanding that those persons appointed to stewardship offices in congregations and denominational headquarters are often rather less than fully "spiritual" Christians. They are not required to manifest the same seriousness of Christian conviction or theological learning as persons closer to the core, the "real work." After all, their task is directly associated with the means, not the end. The qualifications we look for in them are not learning or piety but the kinds of talents admired in the business and professional world. They should be "good at business," and have a knack for public relations, promotional literature, etc. Often such persons are secretly (sometimes not so secretly) scorned. Often they suffer accutely because they know they are scorned.

But even where it is held in higher esteem, stewardship as it is practiced among us seldom rises above this reductionist form. Far from standing for a basic orientation to the world or even a major image of the life and work of the church, stewardship is regarded as a kind of optional ethic for the enthusiastic churchman/woman. People consider good stewardship something private and ascetic, the second mile for which the more zealous church members go in. Tithing! Or perhaps it is held as a more or less acceptable rhetorical sentiment—"We are stewards of all we have . . . etc." Rarely does one encounter Christians for whom the metaphor represents a kind of summing-up of the meaning of the Christian life.

As long as stewardship carries with it such connotations, it is inaccessible for the greater purposes to which it could and should be put today. More than that, it is even possible that unless it can achieve a more expansive and imaginative significance it will not even serve the *functional* goals that it has been assigned for very much longer. There is no reason why stewardship should not *also* have to do with church finances and management. But if it has *only* or *chiefly* to serve these material ends then it will not even serve *them* adequately. The generations preceding ours could be moved by appeals to tithing and church giving and service because it was part of the fabric of their society. It was taken for granted that ministers should be paid salaries, and buildings built and kept up, and organists hired, and missions supported, etc.; and it was therefore assumed that these things had to be paid for by those who believed in them. But none of this is automatic now. If people in or on the edges of our present-day Christian communities are told that they should give of their time, talents and substance, they want to know why. "Shoulds" and "musts" and "oughts" no longer stand alone; there is nothing in the social or ecclesiastical atmosphere to buttress them. Stewardship, even in the congregation and even at the level of finances, must from now on find its rationale at the heart of the faith, as an essential aspect of belief—the end-of-the-matter, and not merely a means to some ill-defined and nebulous "spiritual" end.

4 Enlarging Stewardship Through Theological Praxis

The foregoing critique of the stewardship practices of North American churches does not imply that this long history of stewardship is, after all, of no significance, or perhaps even an impediment to the present call for a broader stewardship vision. It is my strong conviction (a conviction made more firm by frequent opportunities of observing European forms of Christianity that have *lacked* the stewardship tradition) that stewardship constitutes a special and unique *charisma* of North American Christianity. It is not a talent of ours, but it *is* a gift.[8] It has not been kept alive as a concept because it belongs to our nature, our New World genius for self-support and enterprise. It has been given to us through the historical necessities that have made us what we are, that is as a gift.

The point, in that case, is not to make us ashamed of our past by dwelling upon our misuse of the gift. It is true that we have buried it in the financial departments of our churches, and have so domesticated it that it has lost the truly revolutionary quality that it contains. The intention of this study, however, is not to chastise our institutions for having been unworthy stewards of the stewardship idea itself, but rather to remind us all of the breadth and depth of this insight that we have been harboring in our midst almost unaware of its unusual daring. Our task is the elevation and enlarging of the stewardship concept. It exists among us in a state that is somehow dormant, harmless—a matter of good housekeeping. We have made of this revolutionary idea an old shoe that pinches nobody's foot. All the same, it *does* exist amongst us; it *is* at least a familiar term, something of our own, something to build upon!

Building on earlier foundations always involves a bit of tearing down, of course—as Jeremiah well knew when he wrote that the Lord God had commissioned him . . .

> to pluck up and to break down
> to destroy and to overthrow,
> to build and to plant.   (1:20)

Building upon earlier foundations can only be sound and lasting if the rubble and disintegration of the old walls is recognized and cast aside. Theology always contains this critical element, because it is not and must not be done simply out of respect for the past, but out of concern for the present and the future. The *traditions* of stewardship we have inherited are problematic. But they are better than having no traditions at all. The question is, how to benefit from their being there without simply repeating them—building their flaws into our reconstruction of the idea.

Implicitly, we are asking for an appropriate methodology for the study of stewardship; and this quest, in the light of the conern for theological depth that I have voiced in the opening paragraphs of this Introduction, has led me to think that we might learn from the approach explored in many circles today, and especially associated with Third World Liberation Theology.[9] Here, a distinction is made between theory-and-practice, on the one hand, and on the other what is called praxis. The conventional pattern in theology as in many other disciplines has been, first, to enucleate a theory (as in Biblical or Systematic Theology) and then to apply it (Practical Theology, Ethics, etc.). The assumption hidden in this procedure is that thought about reality can occur, and can indeed be more authentic and *true*, if it is removed from act, involvement, practice; that the proper order of things is first knowing and then—as an extension of knowing—doing. Praxis-thinking challenges this ancient assumption of Western, especially European, Christianity. It insists that thinking that occurs apart from the world of involved doing regularly entails an ideological flight from history and the construction of theories about existence that in fact insulate the mind from the real world. Praxis is thought emerging in deed and deed evoking thought. To quote from a recent document—

> Thinking is not now considered prior or superior to action; rather, it takes place in action. The Christian religion was founded not on a word, but on the Word made Flesh. Faith is no longer simply 'applied' or completed in action, but for its very understanding (and this is theology) faith demands that it be discovered in action.
>
> It is necessary to relate Christian theory and historical practice, faith and praxis. Some theologians are talking of a theology defined as critical reflexion on historical praxis. Practice refers to any action that applies a particular theory. Praxis is practice associated with a total dynamics of historical vision and social transformation. *Through praxis, people enter into their historical destiny.* Since praxis changes the world as well as the actors it becomes the starting point for a clearer vision of God in history.[10]

The pertinence of this distinction for our study of stewardship will become evident, I think, if the thoughts expressed in our opening paragraphs here are brought to mind again at this juncture. As North American Christians, it was said, we have not been a theologically profound province of the ecumenical church. Our preoccupation has been with the act, the deed, the *practice* of the faith. Combining this with the next assertion of those opening paragraphs—namely, that sensitive and thinking Christians on this continent are now conscious of the shallowness of a pragmatic faith that lacks a theological foundation—it would be logical to leap to the conclusion, in considering our present topic, that what is needed now is a *theology* of stewardship. This is indeed how many people in the churches, including many who have responsibilities for stewardship programs, are expressing our current need. What is wanted, they affirm, is a sound theoretical basis for the practice of stewardship—something that would lift it out of the merely functional and institutional morass and give it the dignity and directedness of the best Christian *thinking*.

And there is certainly much truth in this felt need. It is even, in a real sense, the implicit direction in which I have been moving in this Introduction.

But there is a danger here, and a very serious one. That danger is pinpointed by the distinction between theory-and-practice, and praxis. Let me put it this way: It would be quite possible to elaborate a fine 'theology of stewardship' that took no real account of the fact that there had been for some centuries a long *experience* of stewardship practice in our own midst. That practice has, as we have duly noted, its real limitations, drawbacks, and impediments. Yet—as we also noted at the outset—it has been the historical vehicle through which a lively image has been at least kept current, and in a manner that it was not current in more theoretical forms of the Faith. Somehow, our *thinking* about stewardship has to incorporate and draw upon that experience, that practice. *Praxis* means that our reflection upon the theological meaning of stewardship involves, not a withdrawal from the practice of it, but "critical reflection on historical practice." A purely theoretical approach to the subject could end by ignoring altogether the lessons that can be learned from our own past, imaginatively revisited.

Accordingly, this study will consciously attempt to be an exercise in theological praxis. That is, in combining biblical, historical, critical, and constructive theological reflection, it will try to think about stewardship in such a way as to help others to "enter into their historical destiny." The *charisma* that we have been carrying about in these so imperfect earthen vessels of our ecclesiastical past and present may, if re-examined in the light of the future use to which it could be put, prove a light to lighten the Gentiles! It was in anticipation of such a possibility that already in the initial paragraphs of this statement I wrote that theological praxis, as distinct from theory alone, must mean reflecting upon our historical practice with sufficient imagination and spirit to wrest from it its deeper meaning— the meaning that, perhaps, only a future moment could fully evoke.

Elsewhere, I have expressed something like the same idea in an illustration. In a recent visit to a Canadian farmhouse attic, I found a beautiful picture, an antique of the 19th century that had been shunted off to the attic by an earlier generation who was ashamed of its old fashioned lines and theme. The family presently living there either did not know about the existence of the picture or else was unaware that, in the meantime, such items were selling like hot-cakes in fashionable antique stores in big cities. The picture was in fact worth far more now than it had originally cost. Ideas sometimes suffer a similar fate. Our theological idea-attic is full, and some of its contents are truly useless and worthless. But there are others, a few at any rate, that are worth more now than they were originally—because in the meantime things have happened to evoke their great importance, usefulness, profundity, etc. Stewardship is, I think, one of those ideas. It has been more or less relegated to the attic (the basement?) by congregations that have grown ashamed of it; but meantime events and attitudes have developed within our world that make it a rather priceless thing. However (to complete the comparison), the best Christian *thinking* in response to those events and attitudes would surely not ignore the picture that had been shipped off to the attic—the idea that had seemed embarrassing or out of fashion; rather, such thinking would be a spirited remembering of that picture, dusting it off, refurbishing the frame, bringing it to light—in short, discovering the beauty and appropriateness that was in it all along, waiting for its right moment, its historical destiny.[11]

5 Ordering Our Reflections

It remains to comment briefly on the ordering of the thought articulated in this short study. We shall begin by considering the biblical background of the stewardship concept—not as an exercise in biblical exegesis alone, but in order to rethink, in the light of the contemporary situation, the origins of the idea. (In other words, the necessary trip to the attic!)

Secondly, we shall reflect on the historical evolution of stewardship. What was the fate of this biblical notion, and what explanations can be given for the fact that it has unfolded in that particular way? (Why was it hurried off to the attic?)

Having in the first two chapters considered the subject in the perspectives of biblical and historical theology, we shall attempt, thirdly, an exercise in critical theology: first (Chapter III) in terms of engaging in a cultural analysis; second (Chapter IV) with a view to identifying the primary religious impediment to a gospel in which stewardship is a major theme. The first part of the exercise in critical theology is necessary because without attempting to discern the signs of the times, difficult as that always is, it is impossible to identify the contextual circumstances that have evoked the 'old idea.' (Why has the picture become a valuable antique?) Theology, Karl Barth once said, means having the Bible in one hand and the newspaper in the other. Already in reflecting on the biblical background of stewardship we shall have had the newspaper in hand; for the separation of content into chapters and the like cannot and should not indicate anything more than a matter of convenience—ordering. But in this third Chapter we shall have to become more explicit about matters already anticipated in the biblical and historical discussions—the things inhering in our present human situation that as it were beg the question of stewardship.

The second part of our exercise in critical theology is more concerned with church than world. The argument here will seek to identify the underlying reason why historical Christianity has been hesitant to pick up and use the metaphor of the steward in its self-understanding. It is my conviction that behind *this* hesitancy there is a much more serious hesitancy—an ambiguity running through the length and breadth of our Christian thinking about the gospel and about our own role in the world. Only if that deeper hesitancy can be pinpointed (Why were we so embarrassed about the picture as to ship it to the attic?)—only then will it be possible to evolve a praxis of stewardship that is more than a shadow of the biblical symbol. Critical theology becomes constructive theology at the point where that degree of honesty and self-discovery has been reached.

Accordingly, Chapter V will attempt a constructive theological statement upon the meaning of stewardship in our present context. And, since such a statement—according to the methodology we have elected—could not legitimately be a merely theoretical one, it will be followed directly by three chapters (VI, VII, and VIII) that are attempts to speak quite explicitly to some of the most urgent issues of that context—issues whose destiny could be altered by a stewardship praxis that had become newly aware and obedient. There is of course no end to the specific problems to which such praxis could address itself. Stewardship is an holistic image of human and Christian obedience; it is universally applicable. But there are areas of our contemporary *problematique* where 'the steward' metaphor has a very direct application. I identify these as The First World/Third World (or North/South) Problem, the Problem of the Human Relation to Nature, and the Problem of War and Peace. My purpose in these chapters will not be to exhaust the meaning of the concept of stewardship, but to illustrate something of its universal relevance by dwelling explicitly on these particular issues.

Finally (Chapter IX) I shall attempt something that theologians probably should leave to their betters and try to answer the question, What does all of this have to do with the living of stewardship in congregations, including the management and financing of their work? I do not intend here to work out a theology of Christian bookkeeping! But if it is true—as I have so boldly asserted above—that stewardship has also to do with budgets and investments and properties, and with the church's mission, then it is mandatory for me to show at least in outline what I believe the enlarged view of stewardship would mean for Christian praxis in these connections. Such presumptuousness must be risked, for the alternative is another exercise in the kind of Docetism I have decried here—the division of the Christian life into "spiritual" and "material" aspects.

BIBLICAL SOURCES OF THE SYMBOL

1 Introductory: Who Is *Ha Adam*?

We begin with the Bible, not simply out of reverence for its authority, but because the steward concept has its origins in these scriptural writings. Parallels of a sort may be found in other ancient religious and mythic sources; but only in the Hebraic-Christian sources, so far as I know, does this conception of the character and vocation of the human creature become a major theme.

This is of course due to the whole "theoanthropology"[1] of the scriptures, and not to the steward metaphor alone. The concept of stewardship in fact only achieves the significant status that it has because it is a metaphoric device for expressing a whole anthropological-theological position. It puts in a word, so to speak, a rather complex but profoundly consistent understanding of the identity, genius, and calling of the human creature, that is of the truly *human* being, of human beings when they are being true to God's intention for them, true to their essential nature.

The Bible is of course full of metaphoric, and also of more literal and technical attempts to capture what the tradition of Jerusalem understands by *humanity*. From simple tableaux like that of Adam as the namer of the other animals to complex ideas like the Old and New Testament's conception of *priesthood*, one finds these ancient writings in a real sense preoccupied with the question, *Who is Anthropos*? What is the essence of this strange, speaking animal? *Wes ist der Mensch*? This is the Bible's primary question—or part of it; the other part of the same question is of course the question about God. But the two questions are clearly inseparable: *theoanthropology*.

As the Bible's question, the question about humanity is not an abstract question. It is not the question of Natural Science, of objective research. The identity and vocation and *telos* (inner aim) of humanity is for the writers of these testimonies an intensely "existential" pursuit. Always, behind the parables, metaphors, images, and theological wrestlings with the identity of this creature there is the bonhoefferian question, "Who Am *I*?" "What is the human creature, that thou art mindful of it?" (Psalm 8) is not the question of a dispassionate observer of "human nature," but the plea of a being who knows that in the universal scheme of things he/she is mediocre and vulnerable indeed! Those who consider that

14

the Bible wants to discuss only the being and glory of *God* fail to grasp the primary motivating thrust behind the whole biblical enterprise, including its modest attempts to depict the Eternal. It is the fact of existence itself that these writers cannot get over. And that does not mean existence in the abstract, but their existence, the existence of Israel, the people that had been no people; the existence of the church, a body that had been nobody, a *creatio ex nihilo* that continues to be conscious of the *nihil* out of which it is being formed. To be a human being is above all, for this literature, to "ask about being" (Tillich); it is to be as a creature who knows that its existence is not *sui generis*; who senses its kinship with the dust, and with the many beings who do not apparently ask about being and are not apparently afraid of not being; who yet feels within itself a yearning and a potentiality that will not permit it to find comfort in the sheer animality of the other creatures. There is in these writings no *independent* interest in the Creator of this and all the other creatures—no speculation (as the Greeks and others have speculated) about God-in-Himself, His existence or nonexistence, His perfections. God in the Bible is the other part of the primary question. He appears at once as the Creator, the Judge, Redeemer, Lord, Saviour, etc. of this questing, questioning being. God is the Answer to the Question that humanity *is*. He is, to be sure, an Answer who more often than not appears in the guise of The Question: a Being who in relation to humanity's 'Who am I?' confronts us with his 'Who am *I*?'—"Who do men . . . who do *you* say that I am?"

The Bible knows with astonishing precision and depth the most prominent answers that human beings have given and, with infinite variations on recurring themes, continue to give to the persistent question of their own being, purpose, and destiny. It knows on the one hand the exalted images that *Homo sapiens* (sic!) has created for the species: that we are gods, or demi-gods, or super men and women; that we are in control of our destiny, full of infinite potential for greatness and answerable to no one; that we are first amongst the creatures, or perhaps tragic figures whose bondage to the dust and the flesh prevents us from achieving the high fate of our spirits, etc. It is aware, on the other hand, also of our strange delight in demeaning and degrading ourselves—of the brand of answers to our existential questions that depict us as low, beastial, worm-like, meaningless, pathetic; a human as "a useless passion," a "sexual twitch" (Sartre), a "nihilistic thought in the mind of God" (Kafka), etc. The Bible rejects both of these *imago homini*. Because its faith is a faith that lives with the Answerer-Questioner, it will not settle for either high or low versions of humanity in which, in effect, everything is decided from the outset—in which there can be no surprises. Against the frequent human attempt to think more highly of ourselves than we ought to think it places the great "I AM" of its Yahweh, and we know that we are dust. Against the equally frequent human attempts to hide in our animality and bemoan our littleness, it presents a God who calls us to stand on our feet and be God's partners in creation!

And so these writings abound in terms, similes, analogies, metaphors, etc., that describe the human condition. And if the reader does not know that the only Answer to the Question of who we are is this other One, this source of Being who calls us into being and gives us our identity, and that therefore no one, final *theoretical* answer can ever be given to that question—if, I say, the reader does not know this about the Bible's fundamental anthropological presupposition, then such a reader might think that the words and symbols and ideas the Bible uses to describe human beings are terribly confused, even contradictory! For we are one minute "unprofitable servants" and the next the very "friends" of God. Here we appear "a little lower than the angels" and there beings whose very *righteousness* is "as filthy rags." Now we are sons and daughters of our heavenly Father, then enemies of Deity, betrayers of God, slayers of His priests and prophets. We are brides; we are harlots. We are lords; we are slaves. We are keepers of earth; we are wastrels and prodigals. We are freedmen/women; we are prisoners. We are self-righteous boasters—hypocrites; we are little children, innocent and trusting. We are oppressors; we are victims . . . etc., etc.

And all of these things about us are true! They are of course not all equally true of everyone at all times—and therefore "The Truth" about us can never be set down for good and all, not even if it is set down 'dialectically'! Because we *live*, and because He lives who has called and calls and will call us into being, there must always be this openness, this possibility of accentuation and variation, this unpredictability. Our existence is a *process*—a dynamic and not a static thing.[2] Therefore the Bible, which wants (as we may say) to bear witness to the *essential* or *intended* being that is always partly present but also always absent and distorted in our existing, has to resort to apparently contradictory ideas and images to identify us. So must theology when it is true to the Bible and to that transcendent Truth to which the biblical writers tried to be true. It must be faithful to the living, the dynamic, the *Sic et Non* that moves in our life, and so avoid at all costs the ideological "defining" of Homo Sapiens which gives the lie to our existence by abstracting certain qualities and potentialities from the whole, ongoing reality.

In the light of this ongoingness, we may say that the best biblical metaphors for the human condition (and the scriptural writers themselves are certainly aware of this!) are those in which the dynamic, the *Sic et Non*, the process-character of life is inherent. This almost invariably means *relational* metaphors: son/daughter; friend; wife/husband; covenant partner; servant; priest, etc. All of these terms tell us something about the possibilities and the limitations of human existence; they contain both a Yes and a No, but in such a way that it cannot be reduced to a principle, a theory. They point to what is essential without turning it into a program, to which living beings must then be fitted. Friendship, for instance, contains certain quite distinctive positive and negative connotations; yet there are myriad ways in which friendship may work itself out in real life—as many ways as there are friends!

It is amongst such metaphors that the concept of humanity as 'the steward' should be placed in biblical thought. It at once tells us something about the No and the Yes of human identity-in-relationship: No, the Adam is not Master; Yes, the Adam is a type of Servant; but No, the Adam is not just a slave, a mechanical puppet; Yes, the Adam is responsible and accountable to Another; No, the Adam is not *just* one of the others; but Yes the Adam is also creature, etc., etc. Yet, while the metaphor points to something essential in the biblical conception of human nature and destiny, it does not itemize or detail this essence. It could not, without being unfaithful to the character of the metaphor itself. There are myriad ways in which stewardship may work itself out—as many ways as there are stewards!

But now we are already anticipating what must be developed more gradually as we consider the specific usages of this metaphor in the Bible.

2 The Hebrew Scriptures

There are some 26 direct references to 'steward' and 'stewardship' in the Bible as a whole. The usage of the term in the Hebrew scriptures is uniformly rather technical or literal; this, however, is where the factual character of the office of steward is developed, upon which its more figurative use in the Christian gospels and epistles depends.

The steward in this literature is a servant—but not an ordinary servant, who simply takes orders and does the bidding of others. He (we do not hear of female stewards here, alas!) is a rather superior servant, a sort of supervisor or foreman, who must make decisions, give orders, and take charge. "*Der Haushalter war ein Sklaye, den sein Herr zum Werwalter über Hausgesinde oder sogar uber seinen ganzen Besitz einsetzte. . . . Sein Amt war eine besondere Vertrauensstellung*"[3] In short, the steward is one who has been given the responsibility for the management and service of something belonging to another.

The 'other' to whom the steward is accountable in the Hebraic writings is usually a royal personage—a king or ruler. So in the first usage of the term (Genesis Chapters 43 and 44) the steward in question is a man accountable to Joseph, the Hebrew prisoner who has meantime risen in the court of Egypt to be second only to the

Pharoah. Joseph's steward is therefore no mean figure. When the brothers of Joseph address this steward, they speak as to one who bears great authority: "Oh, my lord, we came down the first time to buy food . . . .". The steward in turn speaks to them as one who enjoys the full confidence of his master, Joseph. In fact the whole episode establishes a conception of the office in which the steward is really a full *representative* (deputy) of his master.

A less intimate though equally "high" understanding of the steward's office is presented in I Chronicles, Chapters 27 and 28. Here, the stewards who have responsibility for the various properties and aspects of King David's total kingdom (treasuries, vineyards, herds, camels, flocks, etc.) are named, together with the commanders of divisions and leaders of the tribes and the chief counsellors.

A third, brief reference to the steward (in Daniel 1:11, 16) presupposes a similar degree of significance for the office. In this case, the steward is charged, not with properties, but with the care of the young royal Hebrew prisoners of Nebuchadnezzar, and he seems quite at liberty to make immediate decisions respecting them; for when Daniel asks for a radical change in diet the steward complies and, consulting no one, substitutes the desired simple vegetables for the rich royal foods ordered for his prisoners by the King.

This lofty conception of the stewardly office is however balanced by another dimension that becomes visible in a fourth reference from the sacred writings of Israel: Isaiah 22:15f. In this pericope, we learn that, however important the steward may be in the scheme of things, he is neither ultimately authoritative nor irreplaceable. He may be a *superior* servant, but he *is* a servant; and if he forgets this, and begins to behave as if he were himself unambiguously in charge he shall be dealt with very severely. Thus in the passage in question, the prophet is sent to rebuke a certain steward, Shebna—

> "Come, go to this steward, to Shebna, who is over the household, and say to him: What have you to do here and whom have you here, that you have hewn here a tomb for yourself, you who hew a tomb on the height, and carve a habitation for yourself in the rock? Behold, the Lord will hurl you away violently, O you strong man. He will seize firm hold on you, and whirl you round and round, and throw you like a ball into a wide land; there you shall die, and there shall be your splendid chariots, you shame of your master's house. I will thrust you from your office, and you will be cast down from your station. In that day I will call my servant Eliakim the son of Hilkiah, and I will clothe him with your robe, and will bind your girdle on him, and will commit your authority to his hand; and he shall be a father to the inhabitants of Jerusalem . . . etc." (vv. 15-21)

In this reference, the metaphor is elevated to accommodate the idea that the ruler of God's people is a steward responsible to the

Master, Yahweh himself. Moreover, certain qualities of stewardship are implied: humbleness of spirit, lack of pretention and ostentation, "fatherly" behavior towards those for whose welfare the steward is responsible, etc. The leap to a more symbolic usage of the metaphor has not yet been made; but the two poles between which the later New Testament use of the concept moves have been established. One pole—the positive one, if you like—is the close identification of the steward with his master: the steward is, as I have said earlier, almost the representative or vicar of his lord, though he is only a servant. The other (negative) pole is the insistence that the steward is not, after all, the owner; he is accountable to his lord, and he will be deprived of his authority unless he upholds in his actions and attitudes the authority of this Other whom he is allowed and commanded to represent. In the establishment of these two conditions of stewardship, the Hebrew Bible sets up the two most important points upon which all subsequent discussion of the subject turns.

3 The New Testament

The rudimentary picture of the steward as servant-manager of something/someone not belonging to him/herself is also the most obvious meaning of some of the New Testament passages in which reference to stewardship is found (e.g. Matthew 20:8, Luke 8:3, John 2:8). In the Christian writings however there is a certain development in the idea of stewardship. It assumes theological and metaphorical meaning which, while implicit in the Isaiah quotation above, now becomes explicit in certain key passages. Thus in Luke 12:42 ff., where 'steward' and 'servant' are used interchangeably, stewardship together with "watchfulness" are characteristic marks of Christ's true followers. The 'master' referred to here is not an earthly king or lord, but the Christ himself. The disciples, during their Master's earthly absence, are charged with responsibility for his "household". As stewards of their Lord's household, the disciples are responsible for those who dwell there—to see to it that they are properly fed, to keep away thieves, who would rob them of their treasures, to stand watch over their Lord's possessions. But the disciples are warned (in a manner very reminiscent of Isaiah 22) that stewards who forget their place and begin to assume that *they* are in charge, or are at liberty to do as they please with the servants, will be severely punished:

> '. . . But if that servant says to himself, "My master is delayed in coming," and begins to beat the manservants and the maidservants, and to eat and drink and get drunk, the master of that servant will come on a day when he does not expect him and at an hour he does

not know, and will punish him, and put him with the unfaithful. And that servant who knew his master's will, but did not make ready or act according to his will, shall receive a severe beating. But he who did not know, and did what deserved a beating, shall receive a light beating . . .' (vv. 45-48a)

It is true that the stewards are regarded here (as in the Hebraic scriptures) as being a notch higher on the ladder of authority than ordinary manservants and maidservants; but what is from one standpoint their superior authority is from another their greater responsibility. Thus the passage ends with a summary statement that has had great importance for all serious discussion of the meaning of stewardship:

'Every one to whom much is given, of him will much be required; and of him to whom men commit much will they demand the more.' (vs. 12:48b)

Behind this there stands the whole conception of election. Unlike many ancient as well as modern religions and world-views, the tradition of Jerusalem does not think in terms of an elite—the few amongst the many who will be "saved." It is true that the concept of election assumes the choice of a few amongst the many. But these few are "elected," not for their own sake but *in behalf of* the many. They are stewards of "treasures," "food," intended not simply for themselves but for "all the families of the earth" (as it is so beautifully stated in the covenant with Abraham, Genesis 12:1 ff.) The stewards of God's universal grace are, it is true, given "much"; but because what they are given is by no means for themselves alone, "much" will be required of them as well!

In the Pauline and other epistles, the Gospels' parabolic treatment of stewardship becomes almost doctrinal. In I Corinthians 4:1-2, Paul applies the concept of the steward explicitly to himself as an apostle and implicitly to the church at large. One notes again how this reference is set in a context of warning: Christians ought not to act according to the ways of the world, where people try to make names for themselves or form parties around this or that "great" one:

. . . let no one boast of men. For all things are yours, whether Paul or Apollos or Cephas or the world or life or death or the present or the future, all are yours; and you are Christ's; and Christ is God's. (3:21-22)

This is perhaps the supreme ecumenical-ecological statement of the Bible! We are all bound up with one another. No one can claim or have claimed for him or her any independent dignity, authority, or worth. Even Jesus Christ himself is part of this chain of mutuality. Even He is accountable; even He is God's Steward. This being so, "This is how one should regard *us* [i.e. Paul and his associates—but implicitly the church at large]—as servants of Christ and stewards of the mysteries of God. Moreover it is required of stewards that they be found trustworthy . . . etc." (4:1-2). Here the 'property' for which the Christian steward has responsibility is not the material effects of a royal household, nor noble prisoners like Daniel and his companions, nor the accoutrements of a feast as in John 2:8, but "the mysteries of God": that is, of the gospel itself, which is intended for the whole family of *Anthropos*, for God's "household."

This same theological nuance is assigned to the metaphor of the steward in Ephesians. Here however the context adds yet another dimension to the meaning of the steward idea for the early Christians. Paul reminds these Gentile Christians that, formerly, they were "alienated from the commonwealth of Israel, and strangers to the covenants of promise, having no hope and without God in the world"; but now they have been "brought near" through Christ—

> So then you are no longer strangers and sojourners, but you are fel- low citizens with the saints and members of the household of God, built upon the foundation of the apostles and prophets, Christ Jesus himself being the cornerstone, in whom the whole structure is joined together and grows into a holy temple in the Lord; in whom you are also built into it for a dwelling place of God in the Spirit. (2:19 ff.)

And at this point the writer finds it meaningful to introduce the stewardship theme—

> For this reason I, Paul, a prisoner for Christ Jesus on behalf of you Gentiles—assuming that you have heard of the stewardship of God's grace that was given to me for you, how the mystery was made known to me by revelation, as I have written . . . etc. (3:1-2)

The new dimension in this important passage is what we may call the dimension of *participation*. Although the steward of God, like the stewards of earthly lords, can claim nothing for him/herself, that steward is not *merely* an outsider—hired help, so to speak. Rather, the steward participates in the very "household of God." Just as one who participates in this household and its blessings, the steward is called and enabled to share "this grace" (vs. 8) with others and, as Paul has done for his Ephesian hearers, bring them too into God's own household. This in a real sense offsets the other side of the Bible's discussion of stewardship—its negative or criti- cal side—namely the oft-repeated warning that stewards are *only* stewards, and must not arrogate to themselves the posture of owners or masters. While that warning is certainly sustained by Paul, the Ephesians reference to stewardship accentuates the 'high' meaning of the metaphor: the steward is him/herself a *partici- pant* in the very bounty for whose management and distribution he/she has responsibility.

A further dimension is added by I Peter 4:10. It would be appropri- ate for both exegetical and situational purposes to call this *the eschatological dimension* of the stewardship theme in the New

Testament. For here the fundamental assumption is that character-istic, apocalyptic belief of early Christian faith, namely that the End is very near:

> The end of all things is at hand; therefore keep sane and sober for your prayers. Above all hold unfailing your love for one another, since love covers a multitude of sins. Practice hospitality ungrudg-ingly to one another. As each has received a gift, employ it for one another, as good stewards of God's varied grace: whoever speaks, as one who utters oracles of God; whoever renders service, as one who renders it by the strength which God supplies: in order that in everything God may be glorified through Jesus Christ. To him belong the glory and dominion for ever and ever. Amen. (4:7-11)

Whatever else the eschatological context of the Christian life im-plies, one thing that appears prominently in this passage is the way the consciousness of the End reinforces the gift-character of life. Part of what this means, concretely, is that our human tendency to isolate ourselves and our 'talents' pridefully is reduced. The sense of an Ending brings us into a fuller recognition of our own tran-sience, and of our creaturely solidarity. We are all in the same boat—and for faith it is God's boat, God's ark! Here the eschatological and the ecclesiastical presuppositions of the stewardship concept are inextricably bound up with one another.[4]

4 A Linguistic Aside

This is not the place to engage in a complex discussion of the language associated with the stewardship concept. At the same time, we cannot entirely ignore this language—and not only the original biblical terms but also, perhaps even with particular in-terest, the English term that was used to translate the Hebrew and Greek.

The English word 'steward' began to appear in manuscripts in the 11th century. Originally, the word was not 'steward' but *stig-weard, stig* probably referring to a house or some part of a house or all, and *weard* (later, *ward*) meaning of course 'warden' or 'keeper.'[5] The first meaning offered by the *Oxford English Dic-tionary* is thus, "An official who controls the domestic affairs of a household, supervising the service of his master's table, directing the domestics and regulating household expenditure: a major-domo." The dictionary also notes that the word came to be associated in particular with *royal* households.

This, then, was the word available to translators of the Hebrew and Greek scriptures into the English language, including the subsequently so influential King James Version. All things con-sidered, it was not a bad choice—much better, for instance, than many of the *Greek* words available to the early Christians who had to translate essentially Hebraic ideas into the *lingua franca* of that epoch. *Stigweard* in fact approximated quite accurately both the Hebrew and the Greek terms. In Hebrew, a number of terms were employed to convey the office of steward in the four passages to which I have referred above. The Joseph narrative (Genesis Chapters 43 and 44) uses *ha ish asher al* ("the man who is over") or *asher al bayith* ("who is over a house"). Other terms such as *ben mesheq* (Son of acquisition, Genesis 15:2), or *sar* (prince, head, chief, captain, etc., Chronicles 28:1) can also be used.

In the *koinē* Greek of the New Testament, we are taken even closer to the colors of the English word steward. Here, although the term *epitropos* is used in Luke 8:3 and Galatians 4:2, the word regularly translated as steward in most English versions of the Scriptures is *oikonomos*; hence steward*ship* is *oikonomia*. The *oikonomos* has responsibility for the planning and administering (putting into order or *nomos*) the affairs of a household (*oikos*). Not only does this suggest that "economics" (*oikonomia*) is a significant part of Christian stewardship; it means that what we call 'economics' is more than that term usually connotes today. Reflecting upon the word picture as such, we might say that stewardship has not only to do with money, budgeting, and finances but with the whole ordering of our life, our corporate deployment of God's "varied grace" in the life of the world. Beyond that, when one considers that this same *oikonomia* is linguistically close to the term ecumenical (*oikumene*), one has a good deal to contemplate on etymological grounds alone.

5 Theological Reflections on the Steward Motif in Scripture

Language, however, is not immediately revelatory. The word not only reveals, it also conceals meanings. The *idea* is larger than the word, even though the word—in the tradition of Jerusalem particularly!—is of immense importance.

To begin to acquire that larger meaning, we may make certain exegetical-theological observations. It is instructive to order these observations along systematic lines, and so to discuss the scriptural meaning of the concept from the standpoint of its theological, Christological, ecclesiastical, anthropological, and eschatological assumptions. In this way we may begin to sense something of the inclusive character of the metaphor as it is employed in the biblical literature.

(a) Theological Dimension: While the first state in the evolution of the steward concept is evidently the simple idea that there should be someone to manage the affairs of another (king, noble, giver of a feast, *et al.*), the concept easily moves over into a metaphoric meaning. In the first stages of this transition (as in Isaiah 22), it is natural that the 'other' whose affairs the steward is to manage is God himself. The "royal figure" by whom the steward is commissioned and to whom he is accountable is no longer an earthly king but the eternal sovereign.

This simple transfer has very significant implications not only for stewardship in general but also for theology in the restrictive sense, i.e. for our conception of God. It means that ownership, mastery, and ultimacy of authority are attributed *to God alone*. This is of course no novel idea; it gains its power indeed from its absolute consistency with other descriptions of God in biblical literature ("Thou shalt have no other . . ."; "The earth is the Lord's and the fulness thereof . . .", etc.) However, when this is combined—as it must be—with its immediate anthropological implications, it puts a question over all human presumptions, not only in relation to material realities (ownership of properties, etc.) but also with respect to more nebulous realities such as authority. As soon as God is pictured as the owner and master of that in relation to which human beings can be, at most, stewards, institutions such as the holding of property and the hierarchic distribution of authority are thrown into a critical perspective. It does not require a Marx or a Freud to voice that challenge. It is already contained in this metaphor and its attendant theological assumptions.

(b) Christological Dimension: It has been said that the New Testament's theology of stewardship is first a *Christology*.[6] This seems to me eminently true, provided one does not neglect the theological assumption referred to above. Jesus Christ is presented in the New Testament material, not in the role of owner or master, but as the authentic steward: ". . . all are yours; and you are Christ's; and Christ is God's." In a way reminiscent of the whole servant metaphor applied to him, Jesus appears as the steward of "God's grace" who defines and fulfills the office of the steward. Because he is a just and faithful steward; because he desires nothing for himself; because he is obedient to the One he represents; he completes the office in a way that is redemptive for others. Christians, especially in the Calvinist tradition, have discussed the "Work of Christ" in terms of his having fulfilled the three Old Testament offices of Prophet, Priest, and King. They could have used with at least equal justification (and perhaps more beneficially, as a corrective to some unfortunate consequences of what Calvinism came to mean in the area of economics, for instance) the office of steward: Jesus as the steward of "the mysteries of God," lives in such obedience to his stewardly vocation that he becomes both the medium through whom these gifts are distributed to others and the primary model for our stewardship. We are taken up into *His* stewardship. It is not that we achieve the stewardly status through our works; we are graciously brought into a stewarding of God's grace that has been already enacted by this Chief Steward. In other words, the Christological basis of stewardship in the New Testament is this insistence that Jesus Christ, who "is God's," is the initiator and enabler of our Christian stewardship: ". . . you are Christ's; and Christ is God's." The Christological basis of stewardship means not only that our stewardship is *exemplified* by Jesus; rather, in keeping with that Pauline Christ-mysticism that is the matrix of so much of the New Testament's stewardship discussion, it is the prior stewardship of Jesus into which, through the Spirit and faith, we are initiated.

This is very different from a simple exhortation that Christians ought to be stewards. It is the difference between law and gospel, as Luther would say. The *law* of stewardship, which many know to be true enough, insists that human beings must be good trustees of the life of the world. But it is one thing to know this and another to *do* it! The *gospel* of stewardship begins by overcoming that within us that prevents our *being* stewards—the pride of imagining ourselves owners; the sloth of irresponsibility and neglect—and gives us that grace which we need to exercise a love of the world that is larger than our self-esteem or our anxiety. The Christian view of stewardship starts with the stewardship of the One who did not grasp at equality with God, but was obedient (Phil. 2). It is *His* stewardship in which we participate, as those who are brought through the Spirit, through hearing, and through baptism into identity with Him.

(c) Ecclesiastical Dimension: Not only does the stewardship image provide a model for the biblical picture of God and of the Christ, it also quite naturally extends itself into the ecclesiological area of Christian theology. The church is a stewarding community. As those who are *en Christo,* the Christian disciples are being taken up into the work of the great Steward. As "servants of Christ," the Suffering Servant of God, they are being constituted "stewards of the mysteries of God" (I Cor. 4:1) through their witness to the Cross in word and in their own suffering. Their whole life is to be an outpouring of "God's varied grace."

Here as elsewhere there is an implicit polemic in the New Testament against the church as end-in-itself. As we have already observed briefly in connection with the concept of election, which should be seen over against the Hellenistic idea of an elite, the *koinonia* exists for a purpose infinitely greater than itself. It is to serve the God of grace; it is to participate in the extension of that grace throughout the world; it is to be the harbinger of a Kingdom in which it may or may not have a place—nothing can be assumed!

But if there is a criticism of self-preoccupation in the steward metaphor applied to the church, there is an even more vigorous attack upon the ecclesiastical pursuit of *power.* The steward exists not only to serve his master, but (therefore!) to serve those whose interests the master has at heart. When the steward begins to allow his own ambition or desire to dictate his actions, he at once disqualifies himself: "... the master of *that* servant will come on a day when he does not expect him ..., and will punish him, and put him with the unfaithful." (Lk. 12:46)

One could wish that the New Testament writers had developed more fully the *worldly* meaning of the insight that the Church of Christ is steward: how it applied to the Christian community's daily life in the world; how it conditioned our dealings as Christians with institutions like government and economic structures; how it led to an ethic of social responsibility; what it meant for our relation to the nonhuman world, for the 'management' of Nature, etc., etc. As it is, the epistle and gospel writers concentrate almost exclusively on the spiritual and internal-ecclesiastical implications of stewardship: "a bishop as God's steward must be blameless"; the gifts each has received should be shared with others in the *koinonia*, etc. We must remember, however, that the earliest Christian communities were living under conditions significantly different from our own. In particular, their understanding of their mission was conditioned by their expectation of an imminent "End" (see 'Eschatological Dimension'). One of the great advantages of a metaphor like stewardship, on the other hand, is that it is not *bound* to these primitive Christian assumptions, as some other images used in the New Testament to apply to the church are bound (e.g. the 'Bride' imagery of *Revelation*). When the eschatological assumptions change, the steward metaphor is just as applicable as in the earlier situation—perhaps even more so. For there is something questionable about a complete spiritualization of such a concrete and worldly image as this, and in some ways the post-eschatological situation brings the church back to the material and worldly meaning of its vocation as steward. At any rate, it *ought* to have done so! In the next Chapter we shall try to understand why it did not.

(d) Anthropological Dimension: There is no doubt that the New Testament intends us to think of Christians in particular as stewards. It does not develop in an explicit way the idea that human beings as such have a stewardly vocation, any more than it concerns itself with the world meaning of stewardship in general.

This does not however detract from the applicability of the metaphor to humanity as a whole. For one thing, as we have seen, the steward metaphor stands, not alone, but as one of many ways in which the scriptures define humanity's posture vis à vis the Creator and the other creatures. An even more important observation in this instance is that what is described and prescribed in the New Testament as the appropriate life of the followers of the Christ is at the same time the authors' way of discussing "essential humanity" (Tillich), or "man in the intention of God." Christians are not aberrations or suprahuman beings, but persons who are becoming truly human. The 'new humanity' they are 'putting on'—to use Paul's metaphor—is the authentic humanity of Jesus, the *vera homo* (true man), as the Formula of Chalcedon later defined him. God's object in establishing "a people" in the midst of the world is evidently not to create a higher race (an elite!), but through a community being reconciled to Himself and to each other to keep before "all the families of the earth" the vocation and identity He has ordained for us all. As Irenaeus put it so succinctly and beautifully, *Gloria Dei vivens homo* (The glory of God is humanity truly alive).

Though little is made of it, then, the New Testament certainly implies both in its picture of the "true Adam" Jesus and in its discussion of the *Christian* community that is being incorporated into His true humanity, that stewardship is a *human* calling, applying not only to a few but to the species as such.

(e) The Eschatological Dimension: It belongs to the metaphor of stewardship that the one so designated is accountable. It is therefore not surprising that the eschatological dimension should appear so frequently in the New Testament's treatment of this metaphor, as well as in the Isaiah passage implicitly. The Lukan references are especially noteworthy in this connection:

> "Who then is the faithful and wise steward, whom his master will set over his household, to give them their portion of food at the proper time? Blessed is that servant whom the master when he comes will find so doing. Truly I tell you he will set him over all his possessions. But . . . . (12:42 ff.)

The parable of the unjust steward, too, is fraught with eschatological significance. The whole context of that parable is its consciousness of the End—which means, accountability. "Turn in the account of your stewardship!" Stewards must be watchful (Lk. 12), trustworthy (I Cor. 4:2), blameless (Titus 1:7)—not simply out of moralistic concern, but because that with which they are charged is the property of another; it is *God's* grace (Eph. 3:2), and therefore, like the servants who were given "talents" in another parable of our Lord (certainly a cognate reference for any discussion of stewardship), they must finally report on their use or misuse of what they have been given.

This note of the impending judgment (*krisis*) of the steward is, as we have seen, especially the theme of the passage in the first epistle of Peter. The sense of apocalyptic urgency here is not necessarily diminished by the alterations in the *timing* of the Eschaton that necessarily occurred within the first Christian century. It remains true even after the End is no longer perceived as an immediate Parousia that "the judgment begins at the household of God" (as we are told in this same epistle (4:17). Because those who are being incorporated into the life and work of the great

Steward have been given "much," their failure to give "much" in return is especially serious.

In summary, then, we may say that the steward metaphor as suggested in particular by the New Testament appropriation of the Hebraic image, is an inclusive concept, a kind of presentation of the gospel *in nuce.* Indeed it seems to achieve a status beyond the metaphoric. Even though it would be erroneous and exaggerated to consider it a literal or "scientific" description of the meaning of the gospel or any of its aspects, still it possesses a symbolic value that lifts it out of the category of the simple metaphor.

When therefore we speak of the need for an *enlarged* view of stewardship, and when we attempt in the subsequent pages of this study to open up such a view, it is not as though we were simply inventing a new set of ideas and weaving them around an old metaphor. We are rather exploring the depths of a symbol.

Symbols, as Paul Tillich has taught us, unlike *signs,* cannot be invented at will. They belong or do not belong; they are born and they die; but they can neither be produced nor extinguished by us. They are therefore not arbitrary. We receive them as part of the heritage in which we stand as members of a culture or a religion. Their meaning is never exhausted by this or that generation, this or that locale. Because they participate in the reality that they symbolize, their meaning is always unfolding. They are unlike theories in that their meaning transcends every particular expression of their meaning.[7]

The symbol of stewardship belongs to the most ancient strands of our Hebraic-Christian tradition. That much at least is clear from our necessarily brief biblical investigations. Like the other genuine symbols of the Faith, the appropriateness of this symbol is never fully exhausted. No one age of the church, not even the earliest Christians, could have foreseen and fully defined the meaning of this symbol; for its meaning must always be discovered within the categories, the hopes, and fears of successive ages. The biblical writers could see very much about the symbol of stewardship—I have gone so far as to propose that they could anticipate, through it, every *major* dimension of Christian theology. Yet they could not have known the full anthropological-sociological significance of such a concept to an age like our own. They could not have guessed how timely the symbol might become in a world facing apocalyptic issues of the kind only crude myths could hint at for them—a world when the myth of the End is a literal reality with which the human psyche deals daily, but without the horizon of meaning that accompanied humankind's historic mythologies of the end of all things. The depth and appropriateness of this ancient symbol for our own situation must now be explored.

But first—to ensure that our explorations will not be shallow ones—we must ask about the historical fate of this biblical symbol.

Why has it in fact played so minor a role in the unfolding of church history? (How did the picture come to be shipped off to the attic?) If it is truly such an inclusive metaphor as our biblical reflections suggest, how is it that more has not been made of it in the theology and practice of the Christian church?

II REFLECTIONS ON THE HISTORICAL FATE OF THE STEWARDSHIP SYMBOL

1 Introductory: The Aim of the Chapter

It is not my intention here to attempt anything like an historical survey of the course of stewardship thinking in the church, though I believe that such an exercise would be a profitable one.[1] My aim is rather to venture certain historical reflections, which I suppose might be considered hypotheses or, taken together, a comprehensive thesis with various nuances. Naturally such generalizations would have to be tested by more minute and objective historical investigation. Even so it would be difficult to prove the hypotheses I shall develop here: historical generalizations are never demonstrable in the strict sense. On the other hand, the mere review of data without the formulating of some such interpretive hypotheses would amount to an exercise in historical bookkeeping.

2 The Spiritualization of the Concept

During the first centuries of its history, Christianity underwent many changes. The great 19th century historian of Christian dogma, Adolf von Harnack, believed that the transformation was so extensive that what emerged as "the Christian religion" was something quite different from what had been conceived by Jesus and his disciples. Franz Overbeck, the occupant of the chair of Critical Theology at Basel and friend of Nietzsche, went even further: he believed that 'Christendom' was a great mistake, a misunderstanding!

One may not wish to go so far as either von Harnack or Overbeck; still, it is clear that very significant changes did occur, and even scholars who are strongly commited to the Tradition realize that part of the work of Christian scholarship today is to recognize these changes and to recover original meanings that may be both more authentic biblically and more pertinent to our own historical moment.[2]

The general changes in Christian self-understanding occurring during the first four or five centuries of the church had an effect on many if not all aspects of Christian belief, including stewardship. Two eventualities within these centuries materially affected the direction taken by this incipient metaphor of the Christian life: first, the movement of Christianity away from its Hebraic context into the cultural milieu of the so-called Hellenistic world; second, the adoption of the Christian religion by Constantine and his successors as the official religion of the Roman Empire.

The Hellenistic culture, to be distinguished from the Hellenic or Greek civilization as such, refers to that mishmash of Egyptian, Persian, Greek, and other cultures created, largely, by the military exploits of Alexander the Great. This was the arena that early Christianity *had* to enter, as soon as it moved outside the Judaic homeland. Even in that homeland itself it could not escape the influence of Hellenistic civilization. Judaism itself, as one can see from the work of its most renowned contemporary scholar Philo (B.C.E. 20?—C.E. 42?), had been greatly hellenized. Hellenization was so to speak the Americanization factor of the period. While Rome exercised military and political power over the *oikumene* (the civilized world of the Mediterranean area), its cultural values, mores, and goals were set by the earlier Hellenistic civilization. As soon as Christianity became a consciously missionary faith, its representatives, beginning with Paul, had to relate their gospel to the language and the ways of the Hellenistic world. Naturally this meant a partial *adaptation* of itself to the existing culture, for nobody ever shares an idea, experience, or world view without losing some of its original meaning and gaining other connotations that stem from the assumptions of the receiving party. The most obvious aspect of this adaptation process (something still readily traceable) was the manner in which many of the feast days and holy seasons of the pagan, Gentile world were 'baptized' with Christian names and meanings, though they frequently continued to carry the deep undertones of the original pagan festivals.

At a more subtle level, the adaptation of Christianity to the social conditions of the Hellenistic world meant certain alterations in basic tenets of belief. For example there was no word in Greek, the common language of that world, to express precisely what Jesus, Paul, and other Jewish people meant by 'sin.' In the Hebraic tradition, sin means the radical breaking of a relationship—disobedience, rebellion against God, confrontation, and alienation. The Greek word that the Christians did pick up to translate that essentially relational concept (the word *hamartia*, from *hamartanō*) is not a term of relationship but refers rather to personal lack or failure. It means missing the mark, falling short, failing to achieve one's potential, underachieving. Popularly understood, this soon gave way to thinking of 'sin' (sins!) in moralistic and even legalistic ways: sins are wrong thoughts, words and deeds that detract from one's potential for human perfection and goodness. Perhaps that in itself is not an unworthy notion; but it is certainly different from the Hebraic sense of sin as the abrogation of relationship, estrangement. In the

Jewish sense, the trouble with human unrighteousness and sin is not that it takes away from my personal fulfilment but that it introduces 'dividing walls of hostility' between myself and my neighbor, myself and God who is the source and ground of my life. I become alienated from 'the other.' This conception of sin should be borne in mind when we discuss (Chapter VII) the theology of nature; for the other in relation to whom one sins could as well be non-human as human creatures.

To trace the changes in the Faith affecting the theology of stewardship is more difficult because it is indirect. Of course stewardship is also a much less prominent article of belief than a central idea such as sin. With the latter, a failure to find the linguistic materials suitable to the idea at once introduces change. The change affecting the fate of the stewardship symbol was not of that nature; as we have already seen, the Greek *language* could serve that symbol rather well. But there were other, very subtle but ultimately very powerful nuances in the atmosphere of the Hellenistic society, which gave the stewardship idea the direction that it assumed subsequently—or, to put it more accurately, *prevented it* from blossoming in the manner promised by its biblical beginnings.

To grasp this, it is necessary to understand that one of the strongest tendencies in Hellenistic culture and religion was an abiding suspicion of matter. The material world, including of course the human body, was regarded as inferior, the seat of evil, dangerous, and fundamentally *unreal*. To get into touch with the Real, one had to slough off so far as possible one's material attachments together with the passions associated with them. Through such detachment, one might rise to the realm of Spirit. Hence, the function of religion—as well as of most philosophy—was to lift persons out of their 'bondage to the flesh' and relate them to the transcendent, supra-mundane realm of pure spirit. To state it perhaps too bluntly: salvation in the religions and philosophies of Hellenistic civilization tends to mean *salvation from the world*.

By contrast, as even a cursory reading of the Old Testament will show, Hebraic Faith was very earthy! God, for the Jews, was Himself the Creator of the material universe and all its creatures. In the oldest creation narrative (Genesis II), God is depicted actually fashioning the human body with his own hands and blowing breath into its mouth to get it going!—something altogether repulsive to the most representative Hellenistic religion and philosophy. Moreover, the Jews believed (they still do!) that the material world (and therefore also the body and its functions—eating, sexuality, work, recreation, etc.) is "good": "And God saw everything that he had made and behold it was very good." (Genesis 1:31). That evil is also real and terrible was never doubted by the tradition of Jerusalem; but it did and does not locate the source of evil in matter as such. In fact, it regards evil as a product of the human *spirit*, which craves (as we have seen in the foregoing) on the one hand a status "more than" human (pride) and on the other hand settles for something "less than" human (sloth). Matter, in this faith, is the victim of spirit, as it were, not the other way around.

What happened in the move of the Christian faith into the Hellenistic world was that Christianity, which at first was an essentially Jewish offspring, underwent a certain process of 'spiritualization' that robbed it of its potential and essential worldliness. Archbishop William Temple once remarked that of all the world's religions Christianity is the most 'materialistic.' The idea still shocks many Christians, but in terms at least of its origins and the most significant sources of our Faith—especially the biblical sources—it is profoundly true. Christianity takes the material world with complete seriousness: it is both *real* and—in its essence—*good*. But while Christianity shares this conviction with its Judaic parent, the historical evolution of the Christian religion has manifested almost from the start a strong tendency towards an anti-materialistic 'spiritualism.' The story of the church is full of heroes (saints) whose claim to prominence seems chiefly to be that they overcame every *worldly* attachment. An hour's listening to the electronic church of a Sunday morning is all that is necessary to document the fact that this propensity to embrace a spiritualism that in effect despises the world is still very much with us. '*Other*worldliness' is again and again the message of this religion (even though, ironically, the *medium* of this message is as a rule a very crass kind of materialism). This process, which is of course always given a boost by apocalyptic earthly conditions, began with the influence upon our Faith exercised by the religious and philosophic beliefs of the Hellenistic world.

But how does all of this shape the destiny of the meaning of stewardship in particular? The answer, briefly stated, is that it leaves one with a spiritualized version of the symbol; therefore it discourages the development of the stewardship theme as a way of thinking about human existence in its totality, in the psychosomatic unity of its condition. To put the matter more succinctly, the spiritualization of the Christian message occurring under Hellenistic influence meant that a concept with as much *worldly* potential as that of the steward metaphor was not nourished by its environment; it atrophied before it had had a chance to develop; its unfolding was limited to the 'spiritual' side, and therefore the worldly meaning of stewardship remained dormant.

One can readily appreciate how such a spiritualistic reduction of the stewardship motif could achieve a foothold in early Christianity. Remember that one of the most prominent features of the earliest form of the Christian religion was its apocalyptic expectation: "The End is at hand!" (I Peter). As we have seen, this kind of expectancy tended to discourage the early Christians from carrying the stewardship idea into the sphere of everyday worldly responsibility. Although the metaphor of the steward in its biblical expression does contain great potential as a symbol of human responsibility *within creation*, New Testament faith already tended towards a more exclusively 'religious' interpretation of Christian stewardship: as Christians we are stewards of "the mysteries of God," of "God's varied grace," of the *kerygma*. The prominence of "the End" in the consciousness of the early church naturally favored this religious side of the stewardship motif.

But one does not have to indulge in wild conjecture to think that had the culture into which the early church moved in the 2nd and 3rd centuries C.E. itself been more *this*-worldly, Christians as they abandoned, gradually, the most literal interpretations of 'the Eschaton' would have discerned in the steward symbol something having a profound and concrete worldly meaning. There are indeed some hints of this discovery in the writings of the 2nd century Apologists. But the longings of that ancient world, like many of the human longings in our own uncertain age, were not in fact directed towards reconciliation with and transformation of this "good" Earth. People longed, rather, for the permanence, tranquility, and security of life beyond the fluctuations and uncertainties of "this vale of tears." This is what they expected of religion; and this, for the most part, is what they caused Christianity to offer them. Hence the worldly meaning of stewardship was nipped in the bud. Insofar as it was retained in that world-denying, spirit-ladened atmosphere, it was retained in a highly 'religious' form, not infrequently with Gnostic overtones: Christians are the keepers of the secret mysteries of the divine revelation in Christ!

3 The Effects of Christian Establishment on Stewardship

In the Introduction, we have devoted a little attention to the disestablishment of Christianity that has been occurring, with varying levels of intensity, throughout our own historical epoch; and we have noted there that this process carries with it certain consequences for the Christian life that are provocative for the whole question of stewardship. What we have to observe in the present discussion is in a sense the opposite end of that long process, the establishment of Christianity, and the consequences it had with respect to our subject.

If the "dehellenization" (Dewart) of Christian belief is one of the most urgent requirements of our age, the disestablishment of it is the other. It is a mistake to think that establishment meant only external, political changes in the life of the Christian church. The changes occurred also at the level of belief and theology; so that the disestablishment of Christianity entails a great deal of thought and work, not only as regards church polity and pratical issues but in terms of basic understanding of the Faith. Since I have written a good deal about this in other places,[3] I shall not do so here extensively. Suffice it to remind the reader that until the adoption of Christianity by Empire, the Christian faith existed *only* as a voluntary, countercultural movement, embraced by persons at their own risk. Persecution of the church was neither uniform nor always severe during those earliest centuries—exaggerated accounts of martyrdom and the like should be distrusted by anyone who wishes to get at the truth of the matter. Yet to be a Christian prior to 313 C.E. was to opt for a life outside the pale of respectability and against the stream of the dominant culture. All that was changed by the seemingly sudden but nonetheless politically sagacious decision of Constantine to bring the faith of Jesus into the court. Having become a kind of Christian himself, Constantine began to favor our religion politically; and before the end of the same century, Christianity had (under Theodosius) become *the only legal religion of the Empire*!

Now a sociological transformation of this magnitude does not occur without drastic changes at every level, including basic beliefs. I suspect that we are only just at the beginning of the process of historical and theological reflection that is needed in order to unearth the full meaning of Christian establishment. Part of what retards this process is the desire on the part of so many Christians—perhaps most of us!—to *retain* the supposed benefits of establishment. Certainly the effects of this marriage of Church and Empire are to be observed in every major doctrinal area of the Faith. What does it mean, for example, that the most decisive theological formulations of the two most central and complex doctrines of Christianity (Trinity and Christology) were constructed *after* 313 C.E.? The Council of Nicaea was in fact convoked by Constantine himself (325)!

In what way did these changes alter or influence the direction of the *stewardship* motif? Really, in a whole spectrum of ways. For one thing, in the pre-Established situation still assumed by the biblical writers, the Christians had to take direct responsibility for their own life and work. Thus we learn from *Acts* (2:44 ff.) that the earliest Christians "had all things in common." Part of their individual stewardship was this cooperative pooling of resources—a kind of primitive communism that is indeed an aspect of the historical lineage of Marxism. They had to "bear one another's burdens" (as the earliest settlers on the North American continent had to do) because they could expect no outside help, whether from government or private sources. After the establishment of the Faith, however, Christianity became an officially supported cult, and the support extended itself to material as well as more intangible matters.

It does not take a great deal of imagination to realize how such a socio-economic transformation could easily and in a very short time effect changes in attitudes, expectations, and practices. Steward-

ship, for its fulness, depends upon a sense of immediate responsibility on the part both of the individual Christian and of the whole
corpus Christi. When it can be assumed, however, that much of
what is needful for the well-being of the church will be provided by
the state, or simply by the society at large—whether this means
economic support or a constant influx of members, generation after
generation!—then there is no longer any pressing need for incul-
cating such an attitude of personal responsibility in every Christian
or Christian congregation. In any case, it would have been extremely difficult to achieve such an indoctrination; for from the fourth
century onwards the great bulk of those who 'became Christian' did
so as a matter of course, without any fundamental change of heart
(metanoia) or experience of special grace. Indeed, after the reign of
Theodosius (346-395) it was a sheer political necessity to be a
'Christian.' It was illegal to be anything else! This is a far cry from
the Diaspora situation of the earliest congregations—from the
situation of Paul of Tarsus, for instance, an important part of whose
ministry was convincing his converts in the Gentile world that their
new faith obligated them to share their money not only with one another but with congregations poorer and more persecuted than
themselves.

Besides this rather obvious change, the new sociological condition of the church in the established situation brought about very
subtle but very real alterations in the Christian understanding of the
mission of the church. In the pre-established, Diaspora situation,
the Christian community as a countercultural movement was able
to feel a certain solidarity with other oppressed groups and
peoples—with the poor, the political outcasts, the lower classes including slaves, many of whom were the first converts, and others.
Such solidarity is reflected in the parables they remembered (Matthew 25 for example) as well as in the stories told in the *Acts* of the
imprisonment of the apostles, their feeling for other prisoners and
for the oppressed in general. The same sense permeates the literature of martyrdom. Stewardship in this setting *could* mean (not that
it always did) identification with the victims of power, and thus
vigilance for human justice and liberty—a constant theme of the
Hebrew prophets. Under the conditions of establishment however
Christianity permitted itself more and more to be identified with the
dominant political and economic classes of society. As I have put it
elsewhere, the *modus operandi* of the church became the quest for
power through proximity to power. And power-seeking, as we have
seen in connection with our biblical exposition, is no fit attitude for
the steward to cultivate! It belongs to the role of mastery, not of
stewardship. It was quite unlikely that any church bent upon achieving and maintaining a foothold with the powerful would ever *seriously* explore the meaning of stewardship, especially its *worldly*
meaning. Imperial Christianity learned how to use the language of

service; but for the most part this language was more rhetorical and liturgical than real. The church that was inaugurated at the Edict of Milan, unlike the church born at Pentecost, was largely bent upon *self*-service. The losers had become winners by a strange twist of fate, and they quickly demonstrated to the world that they were determined to win everything and everyone—"for Christ," of course!

Fortunately for our present edification and encouragement there were always a few who resisted this ecclesiastical power trip; a few who remembered that "the servant is not above his master;" a few who found power and stewardship incompatible bedfellows. It is chiefly in these that the subsequent history of the stewardship symbol must be traced.

4 Remnants of the Stewardship Motif Amongst the Disinherited

It would be an understatement to note that the two factors named above—the spiritualization of the Faith and its political establishment—have continued to influence the development of stewardship down to our own time. The fact is, the symbol has played almost no role at all in the history of European Christianity. One looks in vain in the great "systems" of dogmatic theology for any mention of the theme. Recently some of the encyclopaediae dealing with Christian faith have introduced articles on stewardship, but still no such definitions are contained in many standard works of this sort—including for example *The Oxford Dictionary of the Christian Church*. It is true that ideas approaching, or cognate to the stewardship motif are developed in major works of theology; but the very presence of these makes one wonder why their authors were not at once drawn to the symbol itself. The reason, I suspect, is that there was very little in the actual life of the church that would have made the symbol meaningful. There is a much closer relation between the practical realities of ecclesiastical life and the themes pursued by theologians than is sometimes appreciated. Having little necessity of pursuing stewardship at the level of their material life, the great churches of Europe had no need, either, to ask about that theme as a theological issue.

It is in fact part of the historical generalization that I am in process of developing here that, in terms at least of the history of its conscious usage, the symbol of the steward must be traced in those groups and movements that broke away from the Christian Establishment, and therefore needed to reorganize their corporate life and their mission in a different way. Something of this can already be observed in the earliest 'break-away' movements, such as the monastic communities, which began to develop shortly after the time of Constantine.

So far as I am aware, the actual use of the term 'stewardship' to describe this alternative to the conditions of established Christianity stems, however, from a later period. In particular it came to designate certain practices in the 'free' churches that came to be along the edges of the Protestant Reformation. It was not, I think, the main Reformation bodies that found this biblical symbol helpful—for both the Reformed and Lutheran branches of the Reformation, despite their radical theology and gospel, continued to espouse an ecclesiology in which establishment was presupposed. There are in both Calvinist and Lutheran doctrine elements that *contribute to* stewardship theology: in Calvinism the theology of covenant is suggestive in this connection, and the theology of Luther, as we shall see later, contains important assumptions for the development of a theology of the stewardship of the natural world. But the steward motif seems not to achieve any special prominence in either of the chief Reformers. It begins, rather, to make a hesitant appearance on the periphery of the Reformation, amongst those not-quite-legal, sometimes rejected and persecuted Protestant bodies, such as the Anabaptists and (later) the Methodists, who unlike the main-line Protestant bodies could not depend upon State or Society for either material or moral support.

This being so, it was natural enough that the most self-conscious and explicit development of the stewardship idea should have occurred on the North American continent. For it was in this New World that the rejected religious bodies of the European parent-society found a place for themselves. They brought two attitudes with them that were fodder for the growth of at least a remnant of the biblical symbol of stewardship: a well-earned suspicion of Christian establishment, and a readiness to assume personal responsibility for the maintenance of free religion—to the point of personal sacrifice.

5 Stewardship in the North American Experience

Even in the New World, stewardship as a specific theme did not *immediately* come to the fore. As Professor Salstrand reports in his book, *The Story of Stewardship*, "In the literature of the colonial period, the term 'stewardship' seems to have no place."[4] The churches in some cases tried to emulate Old World patterns of giving, though this was never very satisfactory. Some of the conditions necessary to the evolution of stewardship practice in the life of the churches had been met in the wilderness of the new continent; other conditions were still awaited.

These latter cannot be dealt with adequately here, for they are part and parcel of very complex historical currents. We may relate them however to two, perhaps antithetical movements in the unfolding of the religious history of the continent. One is the movement called 'secularism.' A consequence of the religious freedom marking the history of North America was the growing awareness of the freedom not to be religious at all, if one so chose. Or, if one preferred a less drastic alternative, one might be privately religious without denominational affiliation. Secularism, whether of the more philosophic sort or simply of the practical variety that allowed one to be a decent citizen without going to church, was I think a condition necessary to the development of stewardship practices in this respect: it provided a background in which it became necessary for the churches to appeal to individual faith and responsibility for the support of the work of the church. Secularism meant that such support could no longer be counted upon as a matter of course; people had an alternative, and a respectable one. In other words we are speaking of the beginning of a disestablishment that reaches far beyond the organizational structures of church and society into the cultural assumptions and beliefs that are the spiritual foundation stones of those structures. One began to develop a propaganda of stewardship at the point where large numbers of the populace, including church members, openly entertained the secular option.

The second movement that provided a necessary boost to the stewardship concept is in some ways the other side of this same coin. We may call it the evangelistic movement, although this term has been rendered unsatisfactory by subsequent usage. What I am referring to is of course the awareness that in a world that offers people the choice *not* to believe and *not* to support the community of believers, the church must work to propagate the faith. It cannot be assumed that belief will occur, genertion after generation, without effort on the part of the witnessing community. Christian witness may be the responsibility of every Christian and therefore the church ought *naturally* to "evangelize"; but practically this does not occur with great success or regularity, and therefore the mission must be organized, must be equipped with the best resources and persons, and must be paid for! Stewardship begins to be a special theme at the point where all these things come together.

Moreover, if the necessity of engaging in an active mission to the world is combined with a growing sense of the this-worldly orientation of the Christian gospel, this too will add incentive to the quest for adequate stewardship practices. Were it only for the "eternal destiny" of the souls of human beings, personal witness might suffice. But if it is felt that the Christian message is meant to bring a better life to people here and now, such a mission cannot be met without funds and without personnel who are highly equipped— medical missionaries as well as preachers, clothers of the body as well as of the soul, teachers of the mind and not only of the spirit.

Those who are more or less acquainted with the history of stewardship in the United States and Canada will realize that I have not arrived at these two conditions for stewardship development arbitrarily. It is not accidental that the "Great Stewardship Awakening," as Professor Salstrand has designated it, occured in the 19th century and in particular in the forties and fifties of that century. For that is also the period in which precisely the movements I have briefly characterized above began to be felt. The secular alternative, which was already well under way in Europe, was of course not the popular route that it has since become in North America; at the same time it was a definite presence, and its very novelty made it seem to the religious instinct all the more threatening. It gave zest and direction to the evangelistic spirit, which, at the same time, was spurred on by the beginnings of that Liberal sense of expectancy that hoped for the Kingdom of God in our time. The shaping of stewardship as we know it occurred in the press and excitement of these days. ". . . . only one more revival is needed," declared Horace Bushnell of Hartford: "namely of Christian Stewardship or the 'consecration of the money power of the church of God.' 'When that revival comes, the kingdom of God will come in a day.' "[5]

6 Conclusion and Transition

In the Introduction, I said that my intention in this study was to engage in an exercise in theological praxis, meaning in part the kind of "critical reflection on historical practice" that enables people to "enter into their historical destiny." In both the biblical exposition of the first chapter and the present discussions we have been considering critically the history of the church's relation to stewardship. What may we conclude at this point that might enable us to move on, in the subsequent phases of the study, to investigate more explicitly the "destiny" that could be present for us in this dimension of our history?

We may, I think, conclude something like this: The metaphor of the steward is sufficiently rich and inclusive in its original conception to warrant being regarded as an important symbol of the Faith, having special reference to the vocation of *Christians* but with implications for the whole anthropology of the tradition of Jerusalem. For a variety of reasons this symbol was not, however, 'selected' by the empirical church in its historical evolving; for most of the history of Christianity it has remained dormant, inactive, even unnoticed.

As the church began to emerge into the modern world, however, the symbol of stewardship gradually acquired currency. It was perhaps inevitable that the power of the symbol was evoked at first by the very *practical* needs of Christian denominations (largely in North America) that found themselves increasingly confronted by the need to develop a biblical rationale for their appeals for financial and other support. Until the present time, the stewardship concept has been largely confined in the churches to this functional office.

But we know from the biblical origins of this concept that the symbol is much larger than the use to which we have been putting it. This we have begun to know, and this incipient knowledge could be the point of entry into *a new phase in Christian stewardship.* Like all great, authentic symbols, the symbol of the steward will permit itself to be used for purposes—including purely utilitarian purposes—that are less weighty than the reality to which it points. But when we take on the use of symbols, even if we do so innocently and merely for pragmatic ends, we open ourselves to the truly profound and sometimes frightening power that they possess in potentiality. The greatest symbol of our Faith, the Cross, ought to have imprinted that lesson indelibly upon our spirits! For the symbol "participates in the reality that it symbolizes" (Tillich), and therefore to associate oneself with it is to open oneself to the awareness of that reality. (Thus the Cross of Christ is the mediatory symbol through which we are exposed to the whole suffering of the world, and of the God who loves it!) *To have begun to know the expansiveness of the symbol of the steward is to have begun to make the transition from the functional meaning of stewardship to a meaning whose proportions and depth most of us, I suspect, have not yet fully anticipated.*

Such transitions cannot be manipulated, they can only happen. We have already observed that real symbols are not invented as signs are. They come to be. Similarly it may be said that the transition from the dormant or incomplete state to something more radical cannot be engineered by us: symbols "grow when the situation is ripe for them." But our increasing interest in the symbol of the steward, our very dissatisfaction with its conventional articulation, accompanied as this is by a growing curiosity about stewardship on the part of sensitive persons outside the Faith—all this indicates that the situation may well be ripe. And if that is so, then no power on earth will prevent this symbol from leaping out of the small, utilitarian harnesses to which we have bound it, and unleashing its power where it is really needed. And we, who are the inheritors of the tradition that produced this symbol—we must either let it go along without us, or prepare ourselves to be carried by it . . . *perhaps* in directions "where you (we) do not wish to go" (John 21:18).

III DISCERNING THE SIGNS

1 A Necessary Risk

This is an exercise in theology, and because theology in the authentic sense is never pure theory but reflection upon our actual involvement in existence, it is necessary to risk decisions about the character of the context in which we find ourselves. Our object is not the preservation of some eternal truth, but to discover how God's living truth is to be understood and appropriated *hic et nunc*. We have proposed that the biblical symbol of the steward has come of age, that the destiny for which our historical experience has been a preparation now awaits it, that the situation is ripe for just this symbol. But it now becomes our responsibility to show *why* such a suggestion can be made. What is the rationale informing it? In what sense is this historical moment one that calls for an openness on the part of the Christian community to the power of this symbol?

Such questions can be undertaken only by a *koinonia* that is prepared to expose itself with sufficient imagination and courage to the unsolved and often appalling issues present in its context. It must open itself to the whole *problematique* of its age—with trust, but without the benefit of ready-made answers, yesterday's answers to yesterday's questions! Above all the *koinonia* must refuse to permit its members, or any who would use it, to make of it a sanctuary against the present. Rather, like Israel and like Jesus, it must allow itself to be led into the wilderness, to be tempted by the demons of its era, unprotected by miraculous and supernatural antidotes to anxiety and temptation. Only so will it discover again the Light that shines *in* the darkness.

Jesus called this necessary risk, "discerning the signs of the times"; and he had harsh words for those religious ones who, in the cause of 'ancient truth,' seemed incapable of discovering what time it was here and now!

But we should not mistake it: there *is* enormous risk involved in the attempt to find out who we are, where we are, what is happening! The risk is not only intellectual, though it is also that of course. Who can with accuracy say what is going on in the present? Hindsight is easier. But obedience in faith is never a matter of knowing what one might have done; it is a matter of believing and deciding what one ought to do now, here. The wise of every age will always judge such 'obedience' presumptuous, because the wise always want to wait until all the facts are in. But of course *all* the facts are never in. (Is that why the wise so seldom act—why for instance European intellectuals in two world wars were so silent?) Obedient stewards of "God's varied grace" must act—unlike that servant who feared his actions might end in the loss of his paltry talent; and so they must be prepared to rush in where the angels of the intellect fear to tread. They must be prepared to hear that they are "fools"—and hope that their folly might at last, through God's transforming grace, serve the cause of ultimate wisdom. Hope that they might be "fools for Christ!"

But the risk of discerning the signs of the times is not only a risk of the intellect. It is a risk of the self, of the spirit-body. For especially in times of great unrest and crisis, the whole inclination of the human heart is to "flee from the wrath to come." By all accounts but those of the most doctrinaire optimists, ours is such a time. The *problematique* of our world is so complex and overwhelming in its scope and ubiquity that it is somehow natural to eschew all contemplation of it. Perhaps the desire to escape from "reality" has never been so strong as it is in our present time. It can be observed (it does not even require special skill in the social sciences to observe!) that the most popular activities in the Western world today are activities that offer the illusion of escape: sex, sports, food, travel, entertainment. Our kind of frenzied preoccupation with such things is incomprehensible apart from the escapism that fires it. And perhaps the most escapist activity of all is religion. The forms of the Christian religion that are most popular today (to the point of displacing traditional Christianity) are those that offer the most effective techniques for escape from history. Whether they do this through 'spiritualistic' flights of fantasy or by the continuous reassurance that there *are* no real crises in the affairs of the world makes little difference. One evades the world just as effectively by eliminating its dark side as by creating a secondary world ("heaven") in which there is no shadow.

There is, however, no genuine escape from time and place. To illustrate: I am writing these words in southern France, inside a house that is perhaps centuries old, situated in the valley of a quiet river and sheltered by ancient hills, far from the tumultuous and violent cities of restless, frightened Homo sapiens. There are moments when, forgetting some of the objects by which I am surrounded (including my Paper Mate pen!) I think myself far away from the 20th century, perhaps with the monks of Cluny in the Middle Ages. But just as I drink in the quietness of such imaginings, the serene Provençal skies are shattered by the vulgar, sickening shrieks of supersonic military jets from a nearby base, and I know that I am a child of the "Age of Anxiety" (Auden). It is in this Age that I must think and do and live. It is this Age that I must try to comprehend if I am to be a steward of God's grace; and to try to transcend this Age is to court the judgment meted out to that unjust steward, who for his comfort decided that the time of his obedience was not yet, and that he might meantime take advantage of the delay of his master.

But how *can* we characterize this Age? Of all the ages of humankind is it not the most perplexing? Who can subject him/herself even to a fraction of the data available in one discipline? The world is full of books that try to tell us who and where we are. Whole institutions, research teams, think tanks, and the like are devoted to the analysis of our society. It is a never ending task, and never wholly successful either. How can we hope to comprehend it?

Certainly we cannot do so in the chapter of a small book. Yet even here we are bound to make the attempt once more. For without coming to terms with ourselves and our times in at least a preliminary way and in relation to the subject we are pursuing here, we cannot discover the *appropriate* expression of this dimension of the gospel. The particularities of our time, we have said, have created an atmosphere in which the ancient steward symbol can come to life. But the life, the shape, and direction our stewardship thinking and acting should take depends upon a more decisive articulation of the character of our time.

2 The Polarities of the Age

Two pervasive attitudes can be detected in our society. At first glance they appear to be opposites—as though a tug of war were going on in the soul of the body politic. But on closer inspection it can be seen that there are connections between the two, that they are not antithetical after all, that one in fact begets and sustains the other. Like so many apparent contradictions, they are in reality of a piece; the logic of their relationship may be obscure, but it is not at all bizarre.

The *first attitude* is what we may designate—what has frequently *been* designated—the technocratic mindset. Let me be quite precise: I am not referring to machinery, not even to the complex and (for average minds) almost magical machinery classified as computer technology. The machinery—those "dark satanic mills" of Blake that in these latter days are often more hygenic and full of light than cathedrals—is nothing but the consequence of a frame of mind. As such it may be frightening enough, especially since so much of the most "advanced" of it is designed for horribly destructive ends. ("Nothing equals the perfection of our war machines."[1]) But what is more appalling is the collective mentality that produces the machinery, sets priorities for its production, and determines the ends to which it is put. It is the technocratic mindset, not merely the technology as such, that must be understood and challenged by all persons of good will. The problematic of our civilization will not be met by Ludditelike striking out at computers or military hardware (even if the symbolic value of such acts may sometimes be great). Chances are, as Kurt Vonnegut so cleverly demonstrates in his fiction[2] and the German and Japanese economic miracles demonstrate in their nonfiction, that even if all the machinery in the world were destroyed it would be remade and improved upon within a generation. What is 'wrong' about us is not our gadgetry, but the attitude towards existence that is expressed in our gadgetry.

Jacques Ellul has defined that attitude in terms of the "systematization, unification, and clarification" of experience:

> . . . technique is the translation into action of man's concern to master things by means of reason, to account for what is subconscious, make quantitative what is qualitative, make clear and precise the outlines of nature, take hold of chaos and put order into it.[3]

Technique is in short the regnant mythology of our epoch. "We *are* technique,"[4] is the simple formula of the Canadian political philosopher, George Grant. Hugh MacLennan has expressed the same judgment in a way that is theologically provocative:

> Technology, which developed as a system of tools and labour-saving devices, greatest of boons to muscle-weary, earth-bound men, now has developed into a kind of universal church with a faith all its own, with a hierarchy of bishoprics and an army of lay brethren known as specialists. Its faith, like the Christian faith in the Middle Ages, is simply this: that its way is the only way to heaven, because it assumes that earth is the only heaven or hell we can know . . . *Vox scientia, vox Dei* . . .

However, continues MacLennan, "despite these miracles, nobody could call the human psyche today heavenly happy or overly confident."[5]

The lack of "happiness," that elusive element the pursuit of which was given modernity's seal of approval in the American Declaration of Independence, can be related to *two concommitants of the quest for technocratic mastery* of the world. One is the loss of any operative sense of meaning or purpose (what the Greeks called *telos*), and the consequent lack of direction conspicuous in the pathetic posturing of the great technocracies. The other is the direct implication of the quest for mastery itself—the tragic flaw in it, namely that when Homo sapiens sets out to master nature he must eventually subject himself, being part of Nature, to the same process of mastery he applies to the natural world at large. Herein lies the connection between the two attitudes to which I have alluded. But before we elaborate on that point, we need to consider briefly what I have named the concommitants of the quest for mastery.

The *loss of meaning* that has been depicted in thousands of novels, plays, and films, and 'celebrated' by existentialism, is the great spiritual fact of our era. Persons who still think and live within the framework of some system of meaning, such as Christianity or Marxism, frequently fail to grasp what it means that for multitudes of human beings throughout this present century there has been no transcendent purpose in existence. Only a few of those who have lived with this sense of purposelessness, to be sure, have had either the courage or the imagination to indulge it overtly, to contemplate it, write about it, express it in song or symbol or word. The majority, as always, has simply lived it—many of them content out of habit to repeat the rituals and proverbs of the past, but in their deeds betraying a spiritual vacuum, a moral wilderness so vast that it is itself the most potent ingredient in our cultural dilemma.

To have lost sight of an horizon of meaning within which personal dreams and ambitions can seem significant is perhaps the most devastating thing that could happen to a people—potentially far worse than even grave physical crises, and certainly the *cause* of many of our physical crises. The loss is crucial for, as Abraham Heschel has so accurately expressed the matter, "Man's vocation is not acceptance of being, but relating it to meaning; and his unique problem is not how to come into being, but how to come into meaning."[6] It is indicative of the primal importance of the sense of meaning for a human community that its loss can be expressed in a symbol like "the Death of God"—though it could as accurately be named "the Death of Man" (as Elie Wiesel and others do in fact name it). If the term 'civilization' has any nonspecific connotation, it is that of a society that is born and that grows on the foundations of some system of meaning; and it is seriously to be questioned whether, in the absence of any such system, human community is possible. Today we are busying ourselves trying to find substitutes for the sense of transcendent meaning, prioritizing our values, and constructing codes of human rights and the like; but it remains to be seen whether any of these self-conscious attempts can stave off the crudity and violence against which they are pitted. Without some foundation in reality (*fundamentum in re*) they appear arbitrary at best, wishful thinking at worst.

> The pre-modern universe was shot through and through with value: there was a hierarchy of purposes into which man with his purposes could fit and feel at home. By contrast, the universe of modern science is a universe of fact without purpose; and because man cannot live without purpose there arises a dichotomy between 'fact' and 'value.' Values are now human only: man finds that he and his values have no counterpart in the world of sheer fact around him—he is radically alone. When Aristotle gazed at the stars, he could regard them as manifesting purposes somehow akin to human purposes. When the Stranger of Albert Camus' novel gazes at the stars, he must regard them as neutral. Thus it seems that man is not only a marginal being within the universe of modern science but also that

his purposes and values, inextricably bound up with any conceivable religion, lack the kind of 'objective' warrant which could be given them by some Archimedian point outside himself.[7]

The consequence for "technique" of the loss of a teleological sense is, to put it in a word (Martin Buber's), that technology is "leaderless." The inventive genius of humanity goes on, of course, even after the demise of meaning. Perhaps it even continues at a pace greatly accelerated in fact, because it knows no boundaries, no limits to growth. But it also knows no goals, no points beyond which it would not be *good* to go. Its progress is directed only by its own inherent voraciousness. Because the thing *can* be done, it *must* be done. Sheer brilliance, curiosity, competition, and the lust for power sweep technology onwards, endlessly—or perhaps towards a catastrophic end that is all too logically bound up with its drive. Walter M. Miller in *Canticle for Leibowitz*, a story set *after* the nuclear holocaust, recalls that the first great Destruction occurred simply because of the unbridled curiosity of a collective technocratic spirit who had lost the capacity for asking about the Good.[8] Those who still today have been given the grace of belief (even if it is only belief in Humanity, or History, or Reason) need to contemplate long and seriously that the world may already be in the grip of forces that are accountable to no belief system whatsoever, that only the logic of 'Progress' remains. "What demons obsess our technology," asks C.F. von Weizsacker, "to make that contemplation impossible to which we ought to turn from time to time if we want to find the right use of technology itself?"[9] That humanity has lost its *raison d'etre* just at the point where it had developed the means to realize some of its greatest dreams is either the ultimate historical irony or the work of a Power that senses again the proximity of the Babel syndrome.

Babel occurred not—as is sometimes naively thought—because Yahweh was *jealous*, but because He was *gracious*. He knew that the pride of mastery leads inevitably to the Fall. The confusion and alienation of a failed Babel is terrible to contemplate; but the degradation of the earth that could be achieved through a *successful* Babel is infinitely worse!

The *hubris* of the technocratic mindset contains a sort of 'Catch 22': Whoever sets out to control the world must sooner or later control the controller; that is, that internal world that is the human spirit must be rendered predictable and harmless. Both the personal and the collective will must be placed under the command of 'the System,' i.e. the rational means by which the chaos and unpredictability of 'nature' can be ordered and its impulsive powers harnessed. You cannot afford to have human beings running about at random, each one pursuing his or her private goals, if your aim is to master and "make history."

The full consequences of this necessity were not noticed until this present century, and there are of course many still (only just prior to 1984!) who have not grasped them. So long as it was possible for the majority to believe in a transcendent purpose in the movement of time, it could be supposed that individual freedom, however self-serving, could only ultimately serve the common good. It was of course this belief that gave the necessary spiritual rationale to capitalism. Adam Smith's "invisible hand" could take the selfish, random deeds of the profit-seekers and make them produce the best of all possible worlds for the majority.[10]

But the disappearance of "objective" purpose,[11] or, to state it in another way, the emergence of the secular society, means that the random or egotistic thoughts, words, and deeds of billions of human beings are not seen to blend nicely into a symphony of order and beauty. Of course, the harmony assumed by the progressive view of history in general and the liberal-capitalist system in particular was always more credible to the rich than it was to the poor; and in fact part of the reason for the disappearance of meaning is precisely the failure of liberalism and capitalism to produce the utopia they promised.

The assumption of the secular, post-liberal world is consequently that the ordering of society, which is no longer accomplished by "invisible" authority, must be achieved by visible authorities, especially states. It makes a considerable difference of course whether the state is influenced by humane ends, and how far it will go towards *compelling* conformity. But what is held in common by most of the states of our present world is the assumption that chaos can only be avoided if order is imposed from above. It becomes increasingly difficult for persons who want to uphold the freedom of individuals to obtain or hold office in *any* of our societies. Even elementary public opinion seems now to be ready to hand over its birthright to whatever Augustus can guarantee *survival*, and it is not overscrupulous about the quality of that survival.

The logic of this mindset has found its most brilliant amanuensis in B.F. Skinner. Skinner is like most of us concerned for the survival of the species. But he believes that Homo sapiens can survive only if a technology of behavior is developed. "Freedom" and "dignity" must go.[12] What we call freedom is in any case only an illusion. We are willy-nilly 'conditioned' creatures. Why not condition people deliberately—for ends that are good, such as social survival, benevolence, and pleasure? So long as we permit the sort of arbitrary decision-making that Western peoples have designated 'rationality' to dominate, we are inviting destruction and oblivion in a society that is beset by the present magnitude of survival problems. Why not permit the true rationality of mastery to be applied to human beings as it has been applied to everything else? This is no time to stop Progress!

The simple fact is that man is able, and now as never before, to lift himself by his own bootstraps. In achieving control of the world of which he is a part, he may at last learn to control himself.[13]

Such logic fits almost to a tee the formula for the kind of *death* of Homo sapiens depicted in the stories of the great anti-utopians from Zamiatin's *We* to Huxley's *Brave New World* and Michael Frayne's *A Very Private Life*. In order to ensure the *survival* of the species, those very qualities that led our predecessors to name our species 'Homo sapiens' are willingly sacrificed! In this recognition lies the transition to the *second* attitude that informs our culture, and that I suspect becomes daily the more characteristic of the two.

When Howard Hughes died at the biblical age of 70, he was reputed to be "worth" more than two-and-a-half-billion dollars, and had become a complete recluse. TIME Magazine wrote ot him:

> In his latter years, Hughes had become the epitome of the 20th century tragedy, a man so preoccupied with gadgets and power that he severed the bond with his fellowmen.[14]

The case of Howard Hughes may be an exaggerated one in certain respects. Few human beings ever amass two-and-a-half billion dollars! But the Willy Loman character of so many of the public figures of our era (so different in this respect from the Carnegies and Vanderbilts of the past) highlights a general malaise, a drama of pathos that is played out silently and unnoticed in the living rooms and offices of our nations. The lives of ordinary people have always been routine and often boring; but in the past, which those of us over fifty can still remember, even the most banal of those lives were provided with a sense of worth and periodic dignity by the conventions, ceremonials, and expressed goals of the community. In the village in which I grew up, there were individuals whose lives were so ordinary and inconspicuous as to seem to provide little more than props on the stage of our youthful dramas; still, these prosaic souls could at least count upon the marriage of a son or the visit of a relative from The City—or at very least on their own funeral—to bring them into some special prominence and even general esteem. All that seems to have gone with the wind. Not only in our cities, where the humble old await their inevitable end in the isolation of hospital wards or rooming houses, but even in the villages that remain, death itself goes unnoticed. Death is unremarkable because life is also unremarkable.

It is as if 20th century humanity had acquiesced quite naturally and without a breath of protest to the absurdly reduced status assigned it by time. The framers of the modern credo could sing the praises of the ingenious being at the helm of the historical process: "Man is the measure of all things." But between their boast and our reality there is a great gulf fixed. The gulf bears the names of Auschwitz, Hiroshima, Viet Nam, and many other events that have conclusively demonstrated the utter cheapness of human life. Societies before ours have known degradation, and their degradation has produced a sense of guilt and shame. But we do not rise so high as guilt. Guilt presupposes the remembrance of righteousness, and in a day when "values" have replaced "goods" righteousness seems little more than an old-fashioned name for old-fashioned morality.

We are small, and there is no undergirding greatness to give our smallness any glory. When the Psalmist "considered the heavens" he felt small, but his smallness did not crush him; for One who was very great was "mindful" of him. When late 20th century Adam/Eve contemplates the vast spaces into which we hurl our costly bullet-like rockets, the sensation produced is very different. Not only the vastly-expanded universe itself, but the very machinery we thrust into it confirms our insignificance. Our own inventions have robbed us of some of the qualities on which we had most prided ourselves. We thought ourselves "rational." But beside the rapid and accurate calculations of the complex computer, our brains seem heavy-ladened. Great seers tell us that our human genius is in any case not to be found in calculation but in meditation.[15] But we scarcely know what thought could mean if it does not mean that calculating which serves mastery. Honoring above all effective technique, we fall short of the canon by which we have come to measure perfection: the perfect machine!

> Every generation has a definition of man it deserves. But it seems to me that we of this generation have fared worse than we deserve. Accepting a definition is man's way of identifying himself, holding up a mirror in which to see his own face. It is characteristic of the inner situation of contemporary man that the most plausible way to identify himself is to see himself in the image of a machine. "The human machine" is today a more acceptable image of man than the human animal.[16]

And lest the reader conclude that this is all in the realm of ideas, let us remind ourselves that "as a people *thinketh*, so it *is*." Our glorification of the machine at the level of spirit and intellect manifests itself powerfully in our daily existence. Unemployment, one of the most devastating problems of most Western societies, is to be traced precisely to this glorification of efficient technique at the expense and denigration of human beings. "Poor people are victimized by the very inventions and machines which improve standards of living for the rest of society," writes Michael Kammen—rather one-sidedly assuming that automation necessarily entails the improvement of our standards of living.[17] The poor are certainly the primary victims of technocracy, but there is also an impoverishment of spirit that in the long haul may be more damaging than material poverty. Unemployment, as well as meaningless employment are symptomatic of a much deeper malaise.

The failure of meaning at the level of public life has resulted in a new privatism that threatens to rob society of those most suitably equipped to serve the public good. This *innere Immigration* has been described by Christopher Lasch as a "Culture of Narcissism":

> Americans have retreated to purely personal preoccupations. Having no hope of improving their lives in any of the ways that matter, people have convinced themselves that what matters is psychic self-improvement: getting in touch with their feelings, eating health foods, taking lessons in ballet or belly-dancing, immersing themselves in the wisdom of the East, jogging, learning how to 'relate,' overcoming the 'fear of pleasure.' Harmless in themselves, these pursuits, elevated to a program and wrapped in the rhetoric of authenticity and awareness, signify a retreat from politics and a repudiation of . . . the past.[18]

To summarize: We find ourselves at the end of a process that began with the Renaissance and expressed itself mightily in the Industrial Revolution: the great thrust forward, the bid for mastery over nature and history. But just as such mastery seems within reach the whole vision has ceased to charm us; it has in fact turned sour. Partly this is because we have sensed a little of the flaw that was in it all along (the 'Catch 22'); partly it is because we have lost, in the meantime, the whole ontic foundation of the vision. We have inherited a dream of glory and we do not apprehend ourselves as glorious. The role was written for someone else, perhaps for Prometheus, as some have suggested—and we are Sisyphus!

3 Old Names for New Phenomena

One does not expect universal agreement with such a portrait of society, and yet I think it is not merely arbitrary or one-sided. Many students of our age have analyzed Western civilization in such broad terms, and I have purposely attempted in this brief statement to incorporate the opinions of many others, especially persons who do *not* speak out of Christian or even religious conviction. This does not of course mean that I have simply set aside my own theological-anthropological presuppositions. But an odd thing about our particular epoch—and incidentally something that makes it quite different from many other periods in the past, especially the 19th century—is that so many of the things traditionally believed concerning the human condition by biblical faith seem so often corroborated today by sociologists, historians, anthropologists, political scientists, artists, and many others who have no interest as such in preserving the Faith.

What we have described above *could* be stated within the traditional categories of Christian hamartiology, i.e., the idea of *Sin*. Sin is not first a category of morality but a category of being. It describes namely the *distortion* of being that is the consequence of distrust, disbelief. And, precisely as in the foregoing discussion, this distortion involves two, apparently contradictory but in reality complementary movements; traditionally the two are named *pride* and *sloth*.

In pride the human creature reaches above itself; it grasps at equality with God—

> So when the woman saw that . . . the tree was to be desired to make one wise, she took of its fruit . . . (Genesis 3:6)

Pride is born of the dissatisfaction with the limits of creaturehood, its lack of permanency, wisdom, and power. Pride is behind the Babel-search for mastery—"Come, let us build a city and a tower . . . lest we be scattered abroad." Sloth on the other hand describes the state of indifference to "fallen" conditions. It means adapting oneself to less than righteous, less than just, less than human circumstances. If pride means reaching too high, sloth means sinking too low. If pride means forgetting that one is human and therefore "capable of failing" (Paul Ricoeur[19]), sloth means adjusting to failure and being fatalized by one's conditions.

It is hard to imagine a society more illustrative of the "state of Sin" so defined than our own! On the one hand we grasp pridefully after a technical mastery of nature and history; on the other hand we wallow in a fatalistic acceptance of our 'destiny,' and slothfully withdraw from the arena of political activity, pursuing our niggardly, private 'happiness.' Pride drives us to pit our inventions and our inventiveness destructively against one another in a build-up of arms that is patently absurd. Sloth keeps us away from the election polls—even so *minor* a public act as that![20]—and convinces us that 'mere individuals' can do nothing to 'change things.' Pride causes us to engage in a collective egotism, a ridiculous and boastful optimism that assigns exaggerated meaning to our space and other achievements. Sloth counsels us in our privacy to cease hoping for any kind of future and to prepare ourselves for oblivion or for hell— hell on earth!

Moreover, the logic of the relation between the two prongs of sin is also wondrously demonstrated in our societal polarities. Sloth is the other side and consequence of pride. It is pride driven to its final state: Since we were not cut out for the Promethean mastery our pride has been seeking, the knowledge of this reduces us to the sulking, disillusioned, and melancholy Sisyphus—"unhappy gods" (Camus). Because we cannot achieve our superhuman ambitions, we seek revenge against the universe in the frenetic pursuit of subhuman pleasures/pains. We have sensed at some deep level of knowing that the vaunted modern dream of human lordship (including that special version called 'The American Dream') has been wrecked on the rocks of 20th century reality. Our response is not unpredictable, if one recollects the ancient dialectic of pride and sloth: We are sinking into a corporate depression. At the rhetorical level we continue halfheartedly to mouth the language of official optimism; but in fact we are losing the capacity to hope.

The old adage affirms that "where there is life there is hope," but human societies before ours have demonstrated that there may be some sort of biological existence without an inherent thrust towards the future. Moreover, Freud has reminded us (he did not invent the idea!) that life also contains a thrust towards oblivion ("the death wish"). The real question that we confront as a society is whether, without any lively and operative hope, there can for long continue to be *life*—real life, not just the semblance of it! "Hope," says the prophetic, drunken priest who is the anti-hero of Graham Greene's *The Power and the Glory*,[21] "is an instinct only the reasoning human mind can kill." Have we been reduced to the necessity of killing our hope in order that we may survive?

4 Stewardship: A Matter of Direct Confrontation

Where does such an analysis leave us in relation to our topic, stewardship? It leaves us, I would suggest, at the very center of the conflict! For if the analysis has any truth, it means that the image and symbol of the Steward can only be explored and put forward today in the form of a direct challenge and alternative to *both* of the postures adopted by our society. Stewardship, rightly understood, constitutes a direct confrontation with the *imago hominis* that informs our culture.

Contrary to the concept of mastery that modern industrial hubris taught us to covet for ourselves, stewardship challenges human beings to assume the posture of *the servant*. Contrary to the retreat from the world into which we have been seduced by our failure to master, stewardship challenges us to a life of *worldly responsibility*.

Thus to "think stewardship" today is to think in very bold terms. It is to be plummeted into the center of the spiritual struggle of late 20th century humanity, the struggle to find a future that is neither the pretentious lordship of the universe that leads with a dread logic to oblivion, nor on the other hand the cowardly slinking away from all thought, planning, and action that aims at change. Stewardship in short no longer concerns itself with matters along the periphery of existence; it belongs to the essence of things. It is for us today very close to what the prophets and apostles meant by "the Word of God." For it is God appearing on the actual scene of our life, as He is so beautifully depicted doing in that quintessentially biblical film, *O God*, and putting to us—insignificant grocery clerks though we be!—the question: Will you at last assume your rightful role in this good creation of Mine? Can you find it in yourselves to take responsibility without being carried away by your own cleverness and power? Can you act the servant without grovelling and demeaning yourselves? You have it in your power to love and to change things! Can you at last take hold of that vocation, without either thinking it too high or too low?

We have seen enough of the biblical and historical background of this symbol to know that it will bear more Truth for us than the church in the past has permitted it to bear. And now we have seen enough of our world to know that the Truth this symbol *could* bear is sorely needed Truth. What we have still to ask is how as a Christian community we might liberate and enlarge the symbol, so that it could achieve the potentiality for radical Truth that it contains for us today.

IV GETTING OUR PRIORITIES STRAIGHT

1 Stewardship and the Revolution of Humankind

Many sensitive Europeans and North Americans have been moved in our times by the plight of the oppressed peoples of the world. Christians can only be grateful for this attitude of solidarity with the poor, wherever we find it and by whatever ideas it is inspired. At the same time, Christian realism recognizes that the condition of the world's oppressed will not be greatly altered until the character of the oppressing forces of our own First World has been confronted, judged, and changed. For citizens of the North Atlantic affluent nations this means: until we have significantly examined and altered our own expectations; until we have ceased to demand of Earth more than our just share of its bounty.[1] Liberation theology is challenging, and it attracts many of our young who are (rightly) bored and frustrated by the business-as-usual mentality of so much "bourgeois Christianity." Liberation theology is a theology of revolution—a theology for those who have fallen among thieves . . .

But we are the thieves. How do you develop a theology for thieves?

It was this sense of the need for a truly critical theology within the First World that prompted one of the greatest exemplars of theological praxis in our time to discourage young idealistic Christians of Europe and North America from seeking their Christian obedience within the Third World context. In 1969, Dom Helder Camara wrote:

> Instead of planning to go to the Third World to try to arouse violence there, stay at home in order to help your rich countries to discover that they too are in need of a cultural revolution which will produce a new heirarchy of values, a new world vision, a global strategy of development, the revolution of mankind.[2]

A cultural revolution! A revolution of mankind! The gentle priest of Recife is no wild-eyed ideologue calling for the violent overthrow of the capitalist system. He is asking, rather, that we white Euro-Americans explore the potentiality of our own best past and present for alternatives to the ethics of greed that have guided our dealings at home and abroad. (I remember well his simple but spirit-penetrating words as he stood before a large audience of students and professors in our university: "Give us a *human* economics! . . . Give us a *human* sociology! . . . Give us a *human* chemistry! . . . etc." He dared to *exhort* in that temple of objective reason!) Dom Helder knows that the only significant revolutions are revolutions that take shape from within the spirit and experience of a people. They cannot be imported. And he knows that apart from such an internalized transformation in our First World behavior and self-understanding, the burdens of his Third World will not be lifted.

There are in fact many facets of our heritage in North America that counteract the exploitation of humanity and nature that has characterized so much of our behavior in the universe—facets which, if they were revived, could create some of the stuff of the indigenous North American revolution for which Third World and other voices are calling. One thinks for example of that fierce determination of our pioneer ancestors, themselves in so many cases victims of oppression, not to import to the New World the noxious distinctions of birth and wealth from which they suffered in the European homelands. Or of that tradition of political idealism that led some of our greatest statesmen and dreamers to envisage a unified society with equal opportunity for all. Or of the spirit of indignation and justice that even if it did not follow through very wisely or nobly, at least freed the slaves. Or of that sense of human interdependence which led to the cooperative movement in Saskatchewan and other Canadian provinces. These and similar aspects of our heritage, in which there is an inherent vision of the common good that curbs the selfishness of fallen egos can, if they are not allowed to be consumed by the rust of collective forgetfulness or the decay of sentimentality, constitute a treasury from which much good can be drawn.

Amongst these treasures, the practice of stewardship is one that is of particular importance to Christians, as we have seen. If it were freed from certain cloying impediments; if it were enlarged to incorporate the radical implications it really does contain, it could become one of the most effective agents for change within the churches and, through their work and witness, in our First World society at large. There is *dunamis*[3] in this symbol. We have shamefully domesticated it, blunting its revolutionary power. Yet it persists, and today it almost openly begs to be set free to perform its revolutionary work in our midst. Moreover, it has one quality that is essential to revolutionary ideas: it is our own. We do not have to import it, as we do so much of our theology. It belongs to our own experience; indeed, it could *become* one of the genuine *exports* of our province of the ecumenical church, if we free it and let it grow.

2 The Basic Impediment

What would freeing the symbol of the steward mean concretely? What impedes its potentiality to effect change?

Many things, of course—some of them, including the function-alist captivity of the symbol, we have already noticed; others shall become the subject of the subsequent chapter. But first we have to deal in basics, and it seems to me that at the most fundamental level what holds back the full revolutionary power of the steward symbol is *a certain ambiguity in our Christian attitude towards THIS WORLD.*

Perhaps this ambiguity belongs to the bedrock, foundational assumptions of the Faith. One can sense it in the Fourth Gospel, for example, that on the one hand presents God's love for the world as the fundamental rationale of the Incarnation and on the other exhibits a permanent distrust of the world and great skepticism about its prospects for salvation. The same ambiguity informs the Pauline corpus. At times, the Apostle can seem very earthy and universalistic in his soteriological pronouncements; at other times he appears to harbor a typical "religious" distaste for matter, flesh, the body, and vows once that as for himself he would gladly depart this world at once and "be with the Lord," as if the Lord were himself not with us *in* the world! Whatever exegetical nuances may be found for such passages of scripture, it would be hard to explain away this certain duplicity in the New Testament's evaluation of the world.

This ambiguity, frequently in practice amounting to a straightforward docetism, presents itself in a prominent way in the history and theology of stewardship. As we have already seen, the great tendency in early Christianity as it moved out into the non-Judaic, hellenized setting of the first and second centuries of the Common Era, was a spiritualization of the kerygma, which meant that stewardship was not allowed to develop its worldly potential. When the church did become "worldly" in the 4th century, it was not the stewardship symbol it pursued and embodied but the symbol of sovereignty. Historic Christianity has seemed either to ignore and escape from the world or else to wish to possess it!

Such ambiguity is at the core of critical thought about stewardship because if we cannot be sure that this world is the immediate object of the divine agape, then neither can we embrace a theology of stewardship that can meet the explicitly worldly demands described in the foregoing chapter.

Nor is this problem one that can be safely assigned to the Christian past! Today the perennial Christian ambiguity about the world amounts to a profound confusion. This confusion has become visible for us in the split of Christianity into two quite distinct groupings or types. The grouping or regrouping has apparently little to do with the older denominational identities and loyalties. It cuts across denominational lines and even across creedal and doctrinal heritages. It seems to me in fact that the real differences between Christians must now be seen in terms of this issue rather than the other distinctions and emphases that gave rise to the various historic splits in Christendom. The point of division comes over two different ways of ordering our Christian priorities:

3 The Theocentric Way

One type of Christianity is clear that its priority is God and the things of God. It thinks that the primary mission of the church in the world is to turn human beings towards the eternal. Its object is the conversion of the unbelieving, or at least that all should be confronted by the claims of Christ and have opportunity to accept or reject them. In its theology, its liturgy, its evangelism, and all phases of its life, this type of Christianity prides itself on being theocentric or Christocentric. That is, it conceives of the Christian life as the cultivation and perfecting of an orientation towards the Divine. This glorification of God does not *always* or *necessarily* entail the denigration of the human and worldly, though in practice it has very often done so.[4] But even where it leads to a more positive attitude towards the world, this type of Christianity makes a clear distinction between obedience to God and the service of the neighbor. What Christians do in and for the world is a second step after their primary duty to God. Those who belong to this camp are very often heard to expatiate on the theme that in Jesus's summary of the Law, the love for God has priority over the love for neighbor, and indeed that the first love (love of God) leads to a kind of love for neighbor that may not be experienced by the neighbor as anything like love. Being translated into practical terms, this very often means that real love for the neighbor must mean doing everything in one's power to convert the neighbor to Christ (an emphasis I have failed to discern in that classical parable in which Jesus defines for us who the neighbor is and what it would mean to love the neighbor!).

There are many variations on this theme of theocentric religion, and not all of those who would embrace the prioritization to which I am referring here would be compatible with one another in every respect. There is a vast difference between the grave doctrinal faith of old Protestant orthodoxy and the bible-thumping vulgarity of the television prophet. Yet in respect to this one issue at least they understand one another—*viz* both represent an *un*ambiguous orientation towards the Divine that results in *ambiguous* attitudes towards the world. Both, too, manifest an abiding suspicion of all forms of Christianity that demonstrate a too *direct* interest in this world. In every one of our churches today there are theocentric watchdogs who periodically warn the fellowship that it is going too far towards Humanism (apparently a very dangerous heresy). Theocentric religion guards against mixing up its priority for God with anything like an equal, simultaneous, or immediate passion for creation.

Today this type of Christianity is very strong. As we have already suggested, it is in fact increasingly perceived as the dominant type—the norm by which "true belief" is measured. Moreover, it would appear that the more *blatantly* theocentric, the more militantly anti-world elements *within* this type of Christianity are increasingly the more dominant. This element has taken the perennial ambiguity of the Christian attitude towards the world and turned it into a rather clear-cut and sometimes pathological abhorrence of the world. For such Christians, the Christian life is a calculated avoidance of this world, with its temptations and evils. It expresses itself in the attempt to create "an alternative Christian environment".[5] So thoroughly incompatible is the sinful world with the life of belief that belief must segregate itself as completely as possible from ordinary life and fashion a world of its own in which everything is consciously "Christian."

The reason for the growing popularity of God-affirming/world-denying forms of Christianity is not difficult to discern. It is almost a rule of history that religion becomes ever more otherworldly during times of worldly crisis. When history becomes incendiary, people look about for fire escapes. This is human, natural, understandable. Every news broadcast in these days must tempt sane minds to flee from burning Rome! But as the legend of the *Quo Vadis*? (not to speak of the Incarnation as such!) has put it so poignantly, *Christ's* way is not out of Rome but into the midst of it!

A final irony of so much of the current religion that is seeking alternatives to the world is that it very often represents no alternative but a mirror image of what it claims to be fleeing from (the chief point of Rifkin's scenario). It turns out to be a variation on the very secularism, materialism, and narcissism it fancies itself to be rejecting. Often it is little more than a coy, stained glass version of old-fashioned North American self-centeredness and isolationism. Thus it is hardly surprising that these types of Christians can join hands with gunslingers and pro-nuclear fanatics to vote into power the most reactionary forces available, sensing that such forces will keep from our doors the beaten, angry, frightened world of the hungry majority and permit us to enjoy our dream a little longer.

4 Christian Humanism

While one grouping of Christians embraces a God-centered faith that in times of global distress expresses itself in ever more bizarre attempts at world-denial, the second grouping centers its attention upon the direction of the gospel. It is convinced that the ethical, world-ward thrust of the Christian faith is the *goal* of true belief and therefore our priority. Working for the transformation of the world is not an option for Christian faith, it insists. Moral responsibility, concern for the neighbor, the betterment of the social order—these things are built into the faith as such. It is not merely a consequence, not a second step. It is part of the first step. You discover God's love as you attempt to love your neighbor. You discover the peace that passes understanding as you immerse yourself in the activities of those who strive for world peace. You find out the meaning of grace as you act graciously towards the ungracious and undeserving. In short, this type of Christianity insists that the human impetus of the gospel is its primary orientation. "The Sabbath was made for man, not man for the Sabbath." The gospel exists for the world, not the world for the gospel! The object of the whole enterprise is not that we should get everyone repeating the Apostles' Creed and intoning "Lord, Lord," but that the *will* of the Lord should be performed in the habitat of those whom he himself befriended: that the hungry should be fed and the sick healed and the imprisoned liberated and the proud humbled and the self-righteous made to know their need for forgiveness and the broken community of humankind reconciled.

It is no secret that the chief intellectual and spiritual power behind this type of Christianity emanates from 19th and early 20th century Liberalism, and in a special sense from the Social Gospel movement, which today enjoys a new comeback here and there. Nor, I think, is it any secret that the stewardship as it is practiced in most denominations on this continent was given a special impulse and direction by the Liberal movement. This is not surprising, for only Liberalism has had the courage or the audacity to answer unambiguously the question I am posing in these pages—or at least part of it: Yes, said the Liberals, Christian people *are* committed to humanity, and that by definition! Other individuals and movements have sometimes approximated such an affirmation. All Christianity has in one way or another insisted that faith must manifest itself in works, must bear fruit. That side could hardly be neglected altogether, even by the most God-enchanted! But at least when it comes to major movements of theology and faith, only Christian Liberalism has dared to say that Humanity is our Christian *priority*: that not even God Himself must be put before the neighbor.

For that reason all of us who wish to pursue the theme of stewardship in something more than truncated forms will retain a healthy respect for Liberalism, with its passion for Christian Humanism. For stewardship can be regarded as a way of being in and for the world only if the human dimension and direction of the gospel is the heart of the matter. I suspect that the return to the study of great Liberal thinkers that can be observed in many theological circles today (including centers behind the Iron Curtain) is to be explained on just such grounds: those who want to put humanity first, as Christians, know that they cannot dismiss Liberalism as easily as this in fact happened earlier under the impact of

Neo-orthodoxy. For only the Liberals were able to embrace an unabashedly *anthropocentric* version of Christian belief.

5 The Inadequacy of Liberalism

It will be obvious from the foregoing comparison that, in respect at least to the ordering of basic priorities, my own sympathies lie with Liberalism. A faith that puts at its center a God who puts at *His* center broken and suffering humanity cannot allow itself to be distracted by the allurements of traditional theism. There is something dreadfully ironic when—as has happened with such regularity in Christian history—people are exhorted in the name of Jesus Christ to embrace a faith in God that insulates them from the pain of God's world!

But while Liberalism takes seriously the human orientation of the gospel of "suffering love," it is nevertheless inadequate as a theological basis for a Christian ethic of radical worldly concern today. Its inadequacy manifests itself at two points in particular: First, in its general assumptions about Humanity and History: second, in its failure to provide the groundwork for an acceptable theology of nature. The first inadequacy has been remarked upon in theology and church ever since Karl Barth launched his attack on Liberalism just prior to the first World War. The second inadequacy however is only just beginning to be recognized, and it is perhaps the more decisive where stewardship concerns today are the issue. We shall examine briefly each of these.

Although the criticism of the Liberal doctrines of humanity and history offered by the great theologians of our immediate past is a lesson that some of us have learned almost too well, there is, it seems to me, a certain need again today to rehearse it. Partly through contact with Roman Catholic theology, which has always been more optimistic about humanity than classical Protestantism; partly through dialogue with Marxism, which as a child of the modern era rejected the biblical concept of radical sin and embraced a version of historical progress that made history as such redemptive; partly simply as a natural reaction against the overemphasis upon the dark side on the part of the Neo-orthodox—for these and other reasons, a substantial trend in contemporary Protestantism appears to have forgotten why Liberalism failed. There is again a danger that those who (in my opinion, rightly) follow in the Liberal tradition of allowing the gospel to make good its human and historical orientation will do so on the basis of a world view that is less than realistic about evil. This danger is only accentuated by the typical North American optimism, which although it is (as we have said) no longer quite genuine, has never known how to handle the experience of negation.

Liberalism in theology failed because there came a day when its assumptions about the *essential* goodness and rationality of the human creature and the progressive march of time towards the divine Kingdom were no longer confirmed by experience; in fact they were, for sensitive Christians and non-Christians alike, totally and devastatingly rejected. The formative events of our century, beginning with "the guns of August" (1914), have rendered the utopian dreams of pre-20th-century humanity inaccessible to us forever. The old categories of sin (even "original sin"!) and the demonic had to be reintroduced into the theological vocabulary to account for what happened already decades ago; and nothing that has happened since then has warranted their being regarded as merely temporary measures! Whoever after Auschwitz, Hiroshima, My Lai, or before "the future Hiroshima" (Wiesel) talks lightly of establishing the Kingdom of God on earth only demonstrates his/her shallowness. That route is closed to us forever. It was in fact never open!

There is of course no doubt that some Christians were too willing to receive the criticism of Liberalism provided by Barth, Brunner, the Neibuhrs, and others. Unlike those great thinkers themselves, many of their disciples settled down into a kind of fatalism about existence: What can one expect in such a world? This too must be fought against mightily by all who seek to develop a responsible theology of stewardship. In other words, *what we must aim for is a theology that is as passionately orientated towards humanity as was Liberalism but that, unlike Liberalism, is perfectly alert to the negative dimension of historical experience.* Our priority must be *this world*, its present and its future; but we can only assume such a priority wisely and with some prospect of its making a difference if we keep our eyes wide open to the extreme difficulty of such an affirmation. What I mean here is stated with her usual eloquence by Hannah Arendt in her essay on Waldemar Gurian:

> His uncompromising realism, which formed perhaps the outstanding trait of his contributions to history and political science, was to him the natural result of Christian teachings. . . . (He had a deep contempt for all sorts of perfectionists and never tired of denouncing their lack of courage to face reality.) He knew very well what he owed to them for having been able to remain what he was, a stranger in the world, never quite at home in it, and at the same time a realist. It would have been easy for him to conform, for he knew the world very well; it would have been easier for him, a great temptation in all probability, to escape into some utopianism. *His whole spiritual existence was built on the decision never to conform and never to escape, which is only another way of saying that it was built on courage.*

The Christian is "a stranger in the world, never quite at home in it" because he/she remembers (and hopes for) a righteousness and justice and peace that the world does not know, though it is of its essence. Yet this homelessness must not tempt the Christian into *other*worldliness, whether of the religious or the secular "utopian" variety, for *this* is the world God loves. The courage to walk between these two pitfalls (conformity and escapism) is a courage that Liberalism cannot now give us.

The second inadequacy of Liberal theology and ethics is only lately becoming visible: that is, its failure to provide an adequate basis for the theology of nature. The truth is, surely, that Liberalism in theology like every other expression of the liberal spirit put the kind of emphasis upon *Humanity* that had in the long run an undesirable effect upon the nonhuman environment that is after all necessary to human well-being. Following the lead of the whole Modern Western mentality from the Renaissance and Enlightenment onwards, theological Liberalism put Man at the center. It even dignified the secular image of humanity as technocratic master of Nature by depicting this wondrous creature as the very crown and jewel of creation. In doing so, the Liberals of course were only taking one side of what had been the traditional Christian view of human nature and destiny. The Reformers also knew how to speak of this "crown and jewel." But Liberalism went far beyond every previous Christian anthropology, both by their praise of Homo sapiens and through neglecting to mention with any consistency the other side of the traditional Christian story: that is, that this no doubt wonderful creature is also full of potentiality for enormous evil, a potentiality that he explores with almost infinite ingenuity! Not only did theological Liberalism refrain from raising any objections over human pillage of the natural universe, but it added to the secular world's celebration of human mastery its own peculiar litanies and exhortations to lordship of the earth. It is thus no wonder that environmentalists like Lynn White, Jr., Paul Ehrlich, and many others growing up in a culture deeply influenced by theological and other forms of Liberalism conceived the notion that Christians are responsible for the ecological crisis.

The question that is put to Christians today (and I have been careful to observe the language of this distinction throughout the foregoing discussion) is not simply, "Do you care about *Humanity*?" It is, "Do you care about *the World*?" Religious liberalism, along with its secular cousins, tended to concentrate so exclusively on *human* worth and dignity that it failed to provide an adequate critique of humanity's encroachment upon the rest of the created order. This was of course part and parcel of its general optimism about humanity. It falls our lot today to work out a theology of radical worldly concern that is aware of both aspects of the Liberal failure. If we are to have an appropriate theology of stewardship, it must be hammered out in the context of an awareness both of the humiliation of humankind and the degradation of nature.

6 Beyond Christian Humanism

What basis could be found for such a theology of stewardship? Liberal theology took shape before the modern world began to get dark. An older form of Christian faith, such as that of Augustine or Calvin, would have said that the world is always dark, that darkness is our condition. But Modernity convinced itself to the satisfaction of everyone except the losers and some of the great poets and intellectuals that all that was past and over. From now on it would grow ever lighter.

Given the general character of 18th and 19th century expectations in Europe and America, it was not asking for a very momentous leap of faith when the great liberal preachers and theologians of that age beseeched their contemporaries to believe in "the fatherhood of God and the brotherhood of man," in "the infinite value of the human personality," in the successive and inevitable progress of history towards God's Kingdom and similar positive things. To go a step beyond this and to ask their contemporaries to align themselves actively with the general kingdom-ward direction of history, to involve themselves actively in the work of the divine Spirit, to become "good stewards" of God's bounty in their conduct of their affairs—this was not asking for something extraordinary, really. In a world that seemed to almost everybody (at least to most of those in church!) eminently prosperous and going the right way, it was not asking a great deal to exhort one's congregation to lend to the process the weight of their own will, effort, and material gains. In fact such a proposal could seem as reasonable as asking one's business associates to buy into an obviously flourishing concern.

But what does today's preacher do? How can we promote a theology of stewardship in a world that from so many accounts seems less than worthy of our best efforts—perhaps already a goner?

One thing is certain: a simple humanism no longer suffices. Without any backing in a more realistic system of meaning, simple humanism, lovely as it often is, falls victim to its own innocency in such a world. Sometimes it ends in despair and narcissistic withdrawal, as we have seen in the aftermath of the activist 1960's. Sometimes it is co-opted by the dominant culture. Sometimes it becomes fodder for the many ideologies, some of them admirable, some violent and frightening, that can seem to give it the backbone it needs in a world that no longer fits its gentle assumptions.

For Christians, the experience of the world's darkening must mean a return to those depths of our Tradition that still understood the dark, acknowledged it, knew that it could not be reckoned with easily, but somehow found the courage to confront it. I am not ready to say that only religious belief can deal adequately with the present shock of historical existence; I have too much respect for profound secular systems of meaning, such as some of the less doctrinaire forms of socialism, to make such a claim. But I do know this: *as a Christian* I am caused by the character of my epoch to search for a reason to be, to be involved, to care, to assume the posture of steward in God's world, that is more clear-eyed about evil and the experience of meaninglessness than simple humanism, including Christian humanism, can be.

What has been for me the most encouraging and even exciting aspect of these recent years—years during which, with my contemporaries, I have been forced to abandon my New World innocency about the world—is the discovery that Christianity does in fact possess unique resources for just this courage. I mean the courage to be honest without becoming hopeless. There are, I believe, in the depths of the tradition of Jerusalem, often hidden beneath trivial and sentimental versions of our faith, sources of truth, wisdom, and hope that were lost to an Age that imagined it already possessed truth, wisdom, and hope in abundance. Recovering these depths, we are enabled to be honest about the world's darkening without losing all track of the light that is given for just that darkness. We may keep our eyes open to the real degradation of creation without letting go of the faith in a God who ''so loved'' it. For the God who identifies himself with this world in our tradition is not a God who is full of power and confidence and above the experience of suffering and humiliation; and the world as it is understood in this tradition is not a world that is always ''getting better and better.'' It is a vulnerable world, forever slipping into oblivion, forever verging on self-destruction; a world on a collision course, not with other planets but with its own spiritual satellite, called by the ancients Hell. And the God who looks with anxious eyes into the dark places of his creation—the eyes of a parent powerless to alter the course of the child's life from *outside* that life—is a God who suffers, who weeps, who is able to break the ultimate power of our Hell only through subjecting himself to it. ''God is dead,'' wrote Friedrich Nietzsche, and we all still smart from that smart remark! But few of us contemplate the second part of the statement: ''God is dead. He has died of his compassion for humanity.'' Nietzsche, I suppose, did not intend that in the way that I choose to hear it: but that does not matter. It is true. Only a God who can be understood to *participate* in a world whose youth listens to songs called ''Don't Try Suicide'' and ''Tragedy'' and ''I'll Never Win'' and the like—only a crucified God could give us the courage to believe that such a world is *nevertheless* worth caring about—perhaps even dying for.

This will I hope make it quite clear that in claiming that all authentic theocentrism is immediately anthropocentric and geocentric I am not opting for mere humanism. Stronger medicine than that is needed for our present day dis-ease. I remain convinced that the direction of the Christian gospel is human-ward and earthward. For that reason I am able gladly to join hands with every sort of humanism. But my own reason for taking up the cause of humankind and earth—as a Christian—will not be found in any humanism, altruism, socialism, etc. It will be found in a faith whose God is the God of Golgotha; a God who is more honest about the darkness of our world than the most determined realist; a God whose light, vulnerable but sufficient, inhabits that darkness before I have even become aware of it. *But* (and this to me is the crux of the matter), woe unto me if I ever turn this *theological* priority into an ethical one! Woe unto me if I regard this faith in God, which is given me as a *means* to worldly involvement, into an end-in-itself. Those who are God-orientated have understood well enough, perhaps, that God is indeed the presupposition of our life and love. But they have become fixated at the level of means. They have not yet found the end. To follow through, they must learn to look where God is looking and to go where he is .... dying of compassion for humanity, for the world.

7 The World Must Not Be Prematurely Abandoned!

To translate the foregoing into the more technical language of systematic theology, what I have been insisting is that the only adequate basis for a theology of stewardship is a newly understood and contextualized theology of the Cross (*theologia crucis*). Since I have written rather extensively about that theological tradition in other places,[7] and since it is a vast subject, I shall not attempt to elaborate on it here, except to say that the fundamental thrust of what Luther named *theologia crucis* is precisely its radical this-worldliness: not in the sense of any easy conformity with or acceptance of this world (after all, it is a theology *of the Cross*), but in the sense of its being rooted firmly in the realities of our life, and its refusal to seek refuge in easy answers to difficult questions. Liberalism was committed to the world—or at least to humanity; but it had not faced the world's deepest questions and impossibilities; it didn't have to. The theology of the Cross leads to a worldly commitment in the face of and in spite of the suffering that such commitment necessarily entails.

Sometimes I think that we have not even touched the surface of the worldly orientation of the gospel of "Jesus Christ and him crucified." Partly this is because Christianity has heretofore been so thoroughly mixed up with ontological and political traditions that had a quite different orientation. Very early in its pilgrimage, as we have seen, the Christian faith became bound up with those Hellenistic and other religious and philosophic traditions that in their zeal for the absolute and their fear of the material world robbed it of its rootedness in the particular and the concrete—*this* world. Then, too, Christianity soon became the cultic playmate of empires and was plunged by these alliances into various forms of plunder in the human and natural communities. Perhaps we are just now emerging from a long, long period of the *misuse* of biblical faith and stand at the crossroads where this faith could become what it is: a religion of worldly stewardship. But this can occur only if we steadfastly and consistently resist the age-old temptation of all religion to conduct its adherents out of history, to provide for them ladders to the gods. The courage and the wisdom to resist this temptation has been given so far only to a few amongst the Christians of nearly 2,000 years. Dietrich Bonhoeffer, in his last years, was one of the most articulate of these.

A few days before he was hanged at Flossenbürg near the German-Czech border, Bonhoeffer was writing to his friend Bethge in the following way—every sentence is vital!

> Now for some further thoughts about the Old Testament. Unlike the other oriental religions, the faith of the Old Testament isn't a religion of redemption. It's true that Christianity has always been regarded as a religion of redemption. But isn't this a cardinal error, which separates Christ from the Old Testament and interprets him on the lines of the myths about redemption: To the objection that a crucial importance is given in the Old Testament to redemption (from Egypt, and later from Babylon . . .) it may be answered that the redemptions referred to here are *historical*, i.e. on *this* side of death, whereas everywhere else the myths about redemption are concerned to overcome the barrier of death. Israel is delivered out of Egypt so that it may live before God as God's people *on earth*. The redemption myths try unhistorically to find an eternity after death. Sheol and Hades are no metaphysical constructions, but images which imply that the 'past,' while it still exists, has only a shadowy existence in the present.
>
> The decisive factor is said to be that in Christianity the hope for resurrection is proclaimed, and that that means the emergence of a genuine religion of redemption, the main emphasis now being on the far side of the boundary drawn by death. But it seems to me that this is just where the mistake and danger lie. Redemption now [in such a view] means redemption from cares, distress, fears, and longings, from sin and death, in a better world beyond the grave. But is this really the essential character of the proclamation of Christ in the Gospels and by Paul? I should say it is not. The difference between the Christian hope of resurrection and the mythological hope [in Hellenistic and other religions] is that the former sends a man back to his life on earth in a wholly new way which is even more sharply defined than it is in the Old Testament. The Christian, unlike the devotees of the redemption myths, has no escape route from history. He knows that this world must not be prematurely written off.[8]

When he wrote these lines, Dietrich Bonhoeffer was only days away from his own worldly omega—at age thirty-nine! In the face of such an end to his own mundane possibilities, he could have been forgiven for taking up, at that juncture, an otherworldly "religion of redemption." Yet here he was, urging his fellow Christians not to take refuge in a form of Christianity that in effect abandons this world. This world, for all its pain and anguish of spirit, in spite of its injustice and cruelty, the deadly competition of the species and their never-wholly-successful struggle to survive—this world is the world for which God offered up "his only begotten Son." It was precisely the belief in a God crucified for the world that gave Bonhoeffer the courage to go to his own death affirming the life of the world.

This, I believe, is where the theology of stewardship must seek its real foundation, and if this foundation is missing then no amount of beating the drum for God and money will make the least difference. If this world is not indeed the first object of Christian concern (I would even say its "ultimate concern"—Tillich), then stewardship of this world is no logical consequence of belief but just an addendum, and we can expect it to be treated as such. But if this world matters, and if the secret of its mattering is felt in the very depths and center of the gospel, then Christian stewardship of this beloved world is of the essence of our belief, and every attempt to shove it off to the side is a form of apostasy and blasphemy.

There are many things that shall have to be accomplished if the theology of stewardship is to take its appropriate place in the community of belief today. But this is the basic thing: the resurrection faith of the people of the Cross means, concretely speaking, that this world must not be abandoned! This, at bottom, is the priority that we have to get straight.

V ENLARGING OUR VISION

1 Principles of Contemporary Stewardship Praxis

The metaphor of the steward comes into its own when Christians grasp that it is *the world* that they are called and equipped by grace to serve and to "keep." This is the first and fundamental tenet, the premise of all that follows. The remaining chapters of this book are nothing more nor less than the beginnings of an attempt to unfold the consequences of such a presupposition. They aim to put together the radically worldly calling of Christian stewards with the explicit character and *problematique* of our context.

We begin this process in the present chapter by identifying some of the basic *principles* that are involved in the enlargement of the symbol. What is meant by "principles" in this connection? It is easier to say what they are not: They are not mere abstractions, deduced from a theoretical pondering of the meaning of the symbol. The methodology of praxis for which we have opted here precludes such a procedure. The principles I shall name in the following discussion (certainly they are not the only ones that *could* be named) have been derived through a reflective process that combines two dimensions: the Christian tradition and experience of stewardship, and the needs of our own historical moment. I would not say that these principles are merely "relevant," because they are at least implicit in the symbol as such, as it was evolved in the faith of Israel and the church. At the same time, neither would I claim that they are eternal, timeless—as theoretical abstractions from the symbol could seem to be. Not every time and place would need to stress these particular principles. It is even conceivable that there could be times and places where some of these principles would be inappropriate. Our time and place on the other hand, as it seems to me at least, *evokes* from the ancient symbol some such conceptualizations as these. It means that the ideas are there, *in* the symbol, to *be* evoked; hence they are not simply arbitrary, superimposed on the symbol by our contextual need for them. At the same time, they must be evoked, called to the fore as it were, by the context. They manifest themselves in the meeting of "Bible" and "newspaper," Tradition and context.

It might be useful to compare this employment of the concept of informing "principles" with what John C. Bennett and others have named "middle axioms." A "middle axiom" in Christian ethics is a principle of ethical reflection that stands between a broad theological-ethical motif on the one hand (e.g. Redemption) and on the other hand the "deed" of redeeming a specific situation, person, group, etc. (e.g. the freeing of slaves). In the case of the examples given here in brackets, the "middle axiom" could be described as the principle of "Liberation." In other words, it is implied in the Christian concept of Redemption, as this is reflected upon by faith in the context of oppression (slavery), that the *liberation* of the oppressed is demanded of those who take the redemption through Christ seriously. The middle axiom of "liberation" is a stage on the way from thought to deed, but it is also a movement from deed (or the arena of the deed) to thought; because without the involved awareness on the part of the Christian thinker in the situation of oppression, it would not occur to him/her that Redemption implies the liberation of the oppressed.

Another quality of the middle anxiom concept that is applicable to what I intend here by the use of the term principles is its accessibility to those who are outside of the faith tradition. Redemption, at least in its explicitly Christian terms, cannot be for those outside the Christian faith the gospel (Indicative) from which they derive their Law or morality (Imperative). We cannot expect the humanists of whom we have spoken in the foregoing discussion to be motivated towards the liberation of the oppressed by the image of the Christ as Liberator or Redeemer. If they are active in movements of liberation (and they certainly are!) it is not because the Christian Gospel of Redemption drives them to such expressions of their faith; it is for many different reasons—for Marxists the Class Struggle, for Liberals the ideals of justice and human rights, etc. Does this mean, then, that Christians cannot work together with these others? Or that, supposing they engage in the same deeds, events, acts of solidarity, etc., they can find no common ground for their labors in the realm of ideas? Such a thing would be sad indeed; for while human beings may of course engage together in a piece of work for purely pragmatic reasons, there is no joy in it—and probably no endurance either!—unless they can find some way of communicating to one another their *reasons* for the work. Horses teamed together do not seem to need any mutually comprehensive rationale for their labor. Human beings do. For 'thinking' is already part of our 'doing,' and vice versa. The middle axiom is a way of speaking about principles that are at the same time fundamentally related to Christian Faith (Redemption) and accessible to many others who engage in protest marches and other activities along with Christians but are 'marching to a different drumbeat.' Both the Christians and the 'others' can communicate with one another around the language of "liberation of the oppressed," and therefore their actual *deeds* of liberation can be achieved in the spirit of joy and solidarity even when the most rudimentary motivation differs from group to group.

I should want to claim the same sort of broad accessibility for the principles I shall name below. I am convinced that they are thoroughly *Christian* principles, that they derive from the Gospel of the Cross, and that they are implicit in the stewardship motif as this motif is contemplated in the light of the contemporary human predicament. But I am equally convinced that they are not exclusively or narrowly Christian. All of them can be—are are!—taken up into the programs and platforms of many others "who are not of this fold." And why should Christians be troubled by such a thing? (Some actually are!) Jesus once had to rebuke his own disciples for that kind of jealousy. Is it not possible, given "the sovereignty of God" and a number of other things in which Christians profess belief, that the hills are full of people who are doing the bidding of our Lord, under many other names—including sometimes the names of those whom Christians fear or distrust?

My principle concern here however is not to show how these conceptions are or ought to be honored by non-Christians. I am writing for those of the household of faith; and, frankly, what concerns me most is that many of our own household seem not to have grasped these principles as well as significant numbers of "outsiders" have! It is our *Christian* vision that I am desirous of enlarging. All the same, one of many benefits that can come to us through such an expansion of the stewardship symbol is that if we allow ourselves to be carried along with the process we shall indeed find ourselves in the company of many others who can also embrace such principles. And there will be great joy in this. It will not be the joy of Babel, which was a false joy based on anxiety and pride; but it may be something approaching the joy of Pentecost, where people began to understand one another a little and could therefore work together.

After we have identified the principles that require our attention today, as stewards of the Great Steward, we shall press on to the deed, i.e. the working out of these principles in three specific areas of our worldly *problematique:* the search for justice for the poor, the search for a more acceptable understanding of the relation between humankind and the nonhuman creation, and the search for world peace. The process of concretizing the symbol of the steward will then, finally, move to a consideration of the implications of all this for Christian persons and for the Mission of the Church.

Thus, once we have made the great leap into worldliness, we are willy nilly engaged in an increasingly explicit attempt to bring the symbol down to earth. This is the logic of the theological praxis of stewardship; it is grounded in the logic of the Cross. The study will succeed only if and insofar as it encourages its readers to carry the spirit and method it has followed ever more exactingly into the quite unique circumstances of their own lives.

2 Globalization

The first principle that emerges in the confrontation of the stewardship tradition and our present day reality is globalization. That for which we have a steward's responsibility is the whole earth.

We have not grasped this. It is true that it is hard to grasp. It's hard to think wholly about anything, including our own persons! If even the microcosm of our own body/soul is difficult for us to get together, this certainly applies also to the macrocosm! No one has ever *seen* "the whole earth." Not even the astronauts who looked at this precious ball of green/blue from on high. To be sure, their image of our planet (i.e. the images of their cameras) has helped considerably to enlarge our vision of that beautiful ball that has been given into our keeping; perhaps that was the most important spin-off of the whole space program. But as even that event in its way demonstrated, becoming aware of the marvellous unity and interrelatedness of the whole earth is not just a matter of *seeing*, in the usual sense. It is finally a matter of belief and acceptance—not without evidence, of course; yet between the evidence and the sense of wholeness there is a leap that has to be made.

And most of us have still not made the leap! With our heads perhaps we understand something of it; but our heart, spirit, gut— or whatever it is that makes our most characteristic decisions at the supermarket and the election booth!—is still living on a flat earth with nicely segregated sections; and this is very nice for those who inhabit the superior sections. We do not think "whole," we think "parts." Rather small parts, indeed!

What strikes me again and again in my travels in North America and Europe (I had a different experience in Jamaica!) is our utter provincialism. We don't even know very much about one another in the so-called *First* World. We hardly care to! We prefer our prejudices to good, solid information. Through the marvels of satellite communications, I can telephone my currently scattered family almost anywhere in the world. But in spite of this closeness of all who inhabit Spaceship Earth, we remain as ignorant of people five-hundred miles away as our untravelled forebears were!

This does not mean that the concern for part of the earth—including "my own, my native land"—is always wrong, or always at loggerheads with global concern and involvement. Indeed, as I have argued elsewhere,[1] I seriously doubt that it is possible for anyone to love the whole without loving this or that particular part. We do not love universals directly; if we love dogs, for instance, it is because we have known and loved and been loved by certain quite specific dogs. To be truthful, I *always* distrust people who say that they love The World, or Humanity, or Nature, or Women. Especially Women! Men who brag that they love women are almost always despisers of particular women, probably chauvinists, and quite possible Don Juans! Who ever meets Humanity? One meets particular men, women, and children. They and they alone are our access to Humanity! Christians and others who speak much about loving Humanity are not infrequently the spiritual equivalents of the male chauvinists who love women. I am not, therefore, proposing that we should all immerse ourselves in a kind of love for The World that would in fact function as a way to avoid loving particular *parts* of the world. There is a kind of "universalism" that is finally just as escapist as any otherworldly religion.

But there is also a narrow particularism that, instead of functioning to put me into touch with something even bigger than itself, keeps my attention riveted to it alone. This is the enemy I am trying to isolate at the moment: this petty parochialism, which like a jealous lover, insists that I should have eyes only for it, for "my own." It is especially obnoxious when it occurs amongst the affluent—which is in fact where it usually occurs (for obvious reasons!). Particular love, if it is really *love*, does not narrow down one's vision; it enlarges it. If what is going on between my wife and myself is really love and not something quite likely closer to hate, then that love will enable both of us to be more (not less!) open to other men and women. Through this particular woman I am given an astonishing gift: the possibility of being open to other human beings who, in my alone-ness, seemed separate islands. The discovery of one love makes more love possible. Isn't that precisely what the First Epistle of John means?—"We love because he first loved us."

All other "love"—all that messiness that tries to get us off in a spiritual corner and keep us for itself—is finally simply untrue. It has no foundation in reality. There are no such corners, away from all "those others."

This is today wonderfully and devastatingly demonstrated by our global unity and ecological interrelatedness. Although we indulge in these divisions (First, Second and Third Worlds; North/South; Rich/Poor, etc., etc.), and although they are historically, sociologically, economically etc. *real*, at another level (not *only* the physical!) they are patently lacking in any ontic basis. They are even absurd, impossible! The globe simply doesn't *have* four corners. Spheres don't! There are no corners around which people can hide and eat their goodies all by themselves forever. There are no walls that can establish a permanent border between this and that part. There are no moats that can keep out the hungry—not even if the moats are oceans! There are no defense systems that can shoot down explosive *ideas* . . .

In short, *there are no parts any more*, if by parts we mean separable entities whose destiny can be lived out in isolation from all the rest. The globe is one, a single creation. It will either survive as one or it will not survive. As a wise and outspoken Moderator of the United Church of Canada (Dr. Bob McClure) once stated it, it is as absurd for First and Second World people to look upon the Third World with unconcern as it is for passengers in a ship's first class to look down on those in steerage and remark, "It seems your part of the ship is sinking," Barbara Ward and countless other sensitive students of Earth have told us repeatedly: You *are* one world. You must learn how to *be* one, or you will not be at all. Today the physical reality of our habitat and all its creatures—a reality that the Hebraic Scriptures sensed long before anyone thought we lived on a sphere!—has become the primal *spiritual* truth by which all our faiths and ideologies and values are judged.

For stewardship, the principle of globalization means (negative dimension) freeing the practice from *localism*, and (positive dimension) learning how to love our own in such a way that that particular love leads us, as it *will*, to the larger reality of which it is part. Our stewardship will be stunted if it settles for anything less than the whole earth.

3 Communalization

A second principle that suggests itself in the juxtaposition of tradition and situation is communalization. The steward in the biblical tradition is first of all not an individual but a community. This does not imply that individuals are excluded; but it means that our personal stewardship is a participation in the stewardship of a community, which, as we have seen, is in turn a participation in the work of the Chief Steward, Jesus. This from the side of the tradition.

But the situation also calls for a communalization of the concept. The sense of frustration that is felt by many of us today as we confront the enormous and apparently unchangeable movement of societies driven by a "leaderless" technology is partly the consequence of that individualism that has been the matrix of our New World experience. At a level deeper than most of us realize, we are conditioned to think that nearly everything worth doing can, may, and must be done by us as individuals. It is as individuals that we must succeed—all the way from kindergarten to a happy and 'well adjusted' retirement. If we fail, we fail as individuals—even though it is patently obvious that the causes of so much individual failure in our society (unemployment, environmental tensions, psychic stress due to overcrowding in cities, that overweeninng sense of purpose-lessness of which we have spoken already, etc.) is attributable directly to societal disorders. The habit of corporate action is very difficult for North Americans especially to learn. Even the pioneer experience, which necessitated the kind of communal cooperation that is here and there still valued, seems on the whole to have given way to the need or desire to make it on our own (which was of course another dimension of the same pioneer spirit). Part of our abhorence of communism is explicable on these same grounds. We manifest an almost adolescent attachment to self-sufficiency, and pathetically imagine that our individuality and freedom would be forfeited if we merged our efforts in a common sruggle.

But this very individualism is one of the chief ingredients in the fatalized attitude that is overtaking us today. Because the forces over against which we must assert ourselves—violence in the cities, scarcity of meaningful work, the threat of war, economic recession, the failure of public institutions, etc.—*are* too great for us to handle as private persons. It is natural to turn one's back on public life and retreat narcissistically into one's privacy—if one bases everything on individual power. But what if we began to think corporately. In 1982 in Western Europe and the United States there are mass demonstrations against nuclear warfare: 300,000 demonstrated in Bonn; 400,000 in Amsterdam; 750,000 in New York City. These demonstrations have already made a difference. The world leaders are all very much aware of this groundswell protest against what seems the inevitability of warfare. Something of this sort began to emerge in North America in the 1960's, too. But it seems on the whole to have given way again to the private quest, and to a sense of futility. There is however *no major problem in the world today that can be confronted without human solidarity.*

A church whose sense of stewardship of the earth included the principle of communalization could contribute much in this situation. Whatever else may be learned from the conflict in Poland between the labor movement, Solidarity, and the government, Christians ought at least to glean from it the lesson that the Christian church can be a forum and rallying point for human solidarity against oppression. Not only that, but one must ask what other rallying points there are! Not only in the officially Marxist lands, but also in our own Free World it is extremely hard to find any place, i.e., movement, organization, or group that can as it were host those who for various and sundry reasons sense the need to look for alternatives. I am not thinking only in the physical or material sense—although even there the point applies: How many of the protesting movements of the 1960s sought space for their meetings in church halls and basements? (Alas, how many were also turned away? But then, some were not). The issue is however much broader: Hosting of the often disparate, often volatile groupings that constitute the search for alternatives doesn't simply mean giving them a place to gather, but creating the sort of atmosphere where something like mutuality can be arrived at. This cannot be done by most of these groupings themselves, because they march to quite specific drumbeats; they adhere to very strict and often mutually exclusive ideologies. Their most natural stance vis à vis one another is distrustfulness, and if they act together it is often for no *positive* reason but for the negative one of a mutual hatred of the status quo. This is, however, no permanent ground for solidarity. Unless an atmosphere of some measure of visible trust is created, the protesting element in every society—often the most important element of the society!—flies apart and fails to act. The dominant forces of all societies know this perfectly well, and count on its happening. A church sufficiently disengaged from the service of the dominant culture and sufficiently open to the prophetic critique of Power could be the prime mover in the creation of 'zones of trust,' where people of many persuasions and hopes could discover middle axioms for their common search.

This is happening more consistently today than it has in the past—and I think that its occurrence is in direct proportion to the effective disestablishment of the church. But we are still much too individualistic in our sense of stewardship. The work of the most significant corporate manifestation of at least Protestantism in the world—i.e. the World Council of Churches—is bedevilled by individualism at the denominational level. Its work cannot be adequately planned in advance, because it can never know whether and to what extent its member churches (particularly in North America) are going to support it. The same thing happens in the denominations and in congregations: Everyone must sit and wait for the Smiths and the Browns to decide whether they are going to give this year and how much. If the "body of Christ" whose members are being knit together to form one body cannot do more to overcome the individualistic nature of so much of our churchpersonship, can we really expect secular organizations like the United Nations to work?

Again then we may say, in sum, that the enlarging of stewardship means (negative dimension) freeing the practice from individualism and privatism and (positive dimension) learning how to realize our oneness in Christ in such a way as to become a genuine community (*koinonia*) ourselves and a forum for encouraging communalization in others.

4 Ecologization

Stewardship means that we are responsible for the globe, and it means that we are *together* responsible for the globe; but, thirdly, it means that our corporate responsibility as human beings for the whole earth includes the stewardship of many creatures, the greater share of which by far are nonhuman. And it means, furthermore, the recognition that the existence of all of these creatures and their environment is a complex state of mutual dependency, so that the fate of one is also in some measure the fate of all the others.

The most problematic aspect of the principle of ecologization will be treated in Chapter VII, where we shall ask after a theology of nature. But here we should introduce the principles as such; namely, the recognition that when we reflect on the tradition of stewardship in the light of our contemporary situation we are bound today to confess as Christians our stewardship, not only of our fellow human creatures, but of the nonhuman creatures and of the whole biosphere that sustains all of us together. It may be argued with some plausibility that this particular principle need not have manifested itself in earlier times; that it is only in view of the crisis of the biosphere that Christians could be expected to perceive such a principle as this. Perhaps. Certainly the multifold crisis of the environment has had to become extraordinarily conspicuous before most Christians took any notice of nonhuman beings. And yet, as I shall want to argue later, there are dimensions in the Hebraic-Christian anthropology generally, and in the biblical symbol of the steward in particular, that point to a long if underdeveloped awareness in our tradition of human responsibility for the biosphere. Some have pointed to the emergence of this awareness in a few individuals—St. Francis of Assisi is a favorite. But there were others, too. Listen to Dostoevsky's "Father Zosima":

> 'Brothers . . . Love all God's creation, the whole and every grain of sand in it. Love every leaf, every ray of God's light. Love the animals, love the plants, love everything. If you love everything, you will perceive the divine mystery in things. Once you perceive it, you will begin to comprehend it better every day. And you will come at last to love the whole world with an all-embracing love. Love the animals: God has given them the rudiments of thought and joy untroubled. Do not trouble it, don't harass them, don't deprive them of their happiness, don't work against God's intent. Man, do not pride yourself on superiority to the animals; they are without sin, and you, with your greatness, defile the earth by your appearance on it, and leave traces of your foulness after you—alas, it is true of every one of us! . . .'[2]

Like St. Francis, Dostoevsky belonged to that tradition of Christian mysticism that believed that all created things have a capacity to manifest the divine (*finitum capax infiniti*). Luther, unlike the reformers whose primary influence was the humanist movement (Zwingli, Calvin) stood in this same tradition. It is not the mysticism that wants to transcend the earth and engage in flights of supra-mundane rapture (what Tillich calls "abstract mysticism"); it is rather the "concrete mysticism" or (as it is sometimes named) Christ-mysticism that plants the feet of its adherents all the more firmly on the earth and gives them a greater love for creatures than they had before. We may say with the authority of this whole mystic tradition that the principle of ecologization *belongs* to our faith! That it is also an overwhelming need within our contemporary situation hardly needs to be demonstrated.

But once again the principle of ecologization can be evoked within the Christian church only with difficulty; because while we may cite Francis and Dostoevsky and Eckhardt and Luther and many others on the side of the animals and plants, we must in all honesty point to a much more powerful "Christian" convention that has been perfectly willing to add the weight of divine authority to the technocratic use and abuse of the nonhuman world. We have already observed that this was a feature of religious Liberalism in most of its expressions. But before Liberalism, indeed from the beginnings of the Modern epoch and the demise of the Middle Ages, there were many avowed Christians who contributed in their way to the evolution of that North American motto (as expressed by Barry Commoner): "If it grows cut it down, if it moves shoot it!" Michael Kammen reports that in 1705, Robert Beverly complained in these words about the Virginians:

> '. . . they depend altogether upon the Liberality of Nature, without endeavouring to improve its Gifts, by Art or Industry. They spunge upon the Blessings of a warm Sun, and a fruitful Soil, and almost grutch the Pains of gathering in the Bounties of the Earth.'

Kammen then reports on William Byrd's *Journey to the Land of Eden in 1733.*, where Byrd discovers a group of land surveyors who had located several large chestnut trees very full of chestnuts. "Our men were too lazy to climb the trees for the sake of the fruit but . . . chose rather to cut them down, regardless of those that were to come after them.' ''[3]

The Medieval sense of an eternal depth in all the creatures of time had given way to a 'thingification' of the natural world that saw nothing in a tree but lumber, paper, or at best, sap. And from the heights of a sort of Protestantism that celebrated the utter *transcendence* of the Divine, this utilitarian attitude towards nature could quite readily find a churchly blessing.

The discovery or rediscovery of the principle of ecologization as a dimension of our stewardship must entail then (negative side) a rejection of all religion that in the name of the Supernatural denigrates the Natural, and (positive) an openness to the mystery of all life, including the willingness to undertake sometimes the sacrifice of our *human* well-being for the sake of the nonhuman.

5 Politicization

The fourth principle that is made necessary by the dialogical meeting of the stewardship tradition with the character of our own epoch is politicization.

Two things could be meant here: First, politicization could mean that stewardship has to be rescued from sentimentality and spelt out in forms that are realistically addressed to the hard political realities of our endangered world. The familiar way of appealing to the spirit of charity and philanthropy in individuals has simply not worked. It is too hit-and-miss. Besides, it has been too consistently concerned to make the philanthropic individuals feel good to achieve any *real* good in the world. As Philip Potter has recently written, "In the past, too much was left to good will and fine statements and it has been shown that it is not enough."[4] The critique of this side of the matter has already been touched upon under "communalization," in our criticism of individualism.

But the politicization of stewardship also points to a second—and even more controversial—issue: namely, the extrication of stewardship from its almost indelible association with economic capitalism.

The truth is of course that stewardship has never been a-political in our North American ecclesiastical experience. It has been subtly married to the politics of free enterprise. In the last century no one endeavored to camouflage the fact! "It is," said the Reverend Josiah Strong, a great advocate of stewardship, "the *duty* of some men to make a great deal of money."[5] He was of course picking up an old theme in North American religion, *viz* the Calvinist-Puritan belief that earthly reward was a sign of divine blessing, and that the tithing of one's wealth was a means of tapping supernatural resources for success.[6] T.A. Kantonen writes: ". . . our stewardship literature abounds in promises of prosperity to those who fulfill their obligations to God."[7] It was this sense of an almost impersonal law of reward that fired the minds of great philanthropists like Andrew Carnegie. As a child who gained much of (I hope) lasting benefit from hours spent in a Carnegie endowed public library, I should be the last to question that such philanthropists often contributed substantially to the life of the community. But we are not judging people here, but a principle: and the ill effects of the association of Christian stewardship with the philanthropy of religious capitalists have been far reaching.

Already in 1930, Reinhold Niebuhr, noticing these ill effects, wrote an article for *The Christian Century* provocatively entitled, "Is Stewardship Enough?" Niebuhr's argument is if anything more valid today, given the fact of multi-nationals and income tax reductions for contributions to charity, than it was in 1930. He said that "philanthropy is not stewardship," and that when it was passed off as stewardship it in fact frequently covered up a great deal of injustice perpetrated by the same Christian philanthropists who were held up as models of charity. "How inadequate" our alleged stewardship is, he wrote, . . .

... may be recognized from the fact that in the year 1929 the total philanthropies of America amounted to two and a half billion dollars, a sum that does not equal the accretion of values in stocks on the New York exchange in a single day . . . . It is, of course, not impossible to interpret the doctrine of stewardship realistically. But to do so would require an honest discussion of every moral and social problem involved in modern industry, the displacement of workers by the machine, the inequality of income, the ethics of varying standards of living, the democratic rights of workers, and all the rest. If this is not done, it is idle to think of the church as a moral guide in our civilization.[8]

As Niebuhr implies, the politicization—rather, the re-politicization—of stewardship may involve the churches in a new look at the socialist alternative to capitalism. Surely it is no longer radical to suggest such a thing. Even a study as mild in its critical cultural appraisal as that of Holmes Rolston[9] presents a similar proposal. Commenting upon the "Differing Forms of the Economic Order" present in our contemporary world, Rolston notes that . . .

... the very fact that millions of men do live under an economic order which is radically different from our own must raise even in the mind of the most unthinking Christian some questions as to the permanence of the form of the economic order within which he lives.[10]

While it is true that "Many of the great fortunes of North America have been dedicated, in part at least, to the great causes of human welfare," still "the Christian faith is not identified with the preservation of the existing form of the economic order." Of course, there will always be subtle attempts on the part of those who benefit from the economic order to lend it supernatural sanction. ". . . there will always be pressure exerted upon the church to identify Christianity with the preservation of the economic order in its existing form . . .

From this point of view, the history of Christianity often makes painful reading. Men have sought to throw the whole power of the church behind the preservation of slavery in America, or the tyranny of the feudalism of Russia, or the interests of the landed aristocracy of Spain.[11]

It is just possible, Rolston concludes, that Christians could eventually find socialized forms of the economic-political order more compatible with basic Christian beliefs than the older forms with which the church of the centuries has been yoked:

Christianity has lived with slavery, and feudalism, and capitalism. She may learn to live in the more socialized forms of society towards which modern society seems to be moving. In fact, she may find some of the newer forms of society more congenial to her life than the more ancient forms of the economic order. In this respect, Christianity must judge all orders of society. She must point to the evils in the existing economic order. She must be prepared also to examine from the point of view of the insights of the Christian any form of the economic order which may be established in the future.[12]

This summarizes the principle I am discussing here. It is not a matter of all Christians becoming doctrinaire socialists! Christians will always have to be prophetically vigilant, no matter what the social order. But it is a matter, surely, of a more critical stance vis a vis the alliance of Christianity and economic capitalism. That is the negative dimension of the politicization of stewardship: we must call in question the subtle identification of Christian faith and life and the political-economic assumptions of the free enterprise system. And on the positive side, politicization means the search for new forms of community—including a 'New Economic Order'— that can more adequately reflect our faith's concern for justice, equality, and mercy.

6 Futurization

The final principle that I shall name here (I leave it to the reader to continue this search) is what I should call the principle of futurization. Stewardship means that we are responsible for the whole earth (first principle); that we are *together* responsible for the whole earth (second principle); that this responsibility includes the non-human as well as the human world (third principle); that this responsibility must seek to express itself in just and merciful political forms (fourth principle)—and (fifth principle) that this responsibility must be exercised in the light, not only of the immediate present but of the future as well.

Have you noticed the high consciousness of the future in the Hebraic scriptures? They are always speaking about "the children's children", and "unto the third and fourth generation," and way beyond. This future orientation almost disappears in the New Testament—or, rather, it is redirected. There it becomes a heavenly future, or the future of the new order inaugurated by the Christ—the Kingdom. This of course has important implications for stewardship, too, as we have seen in our discussion of the eschatological dimension. But an unfortunate effect of the New Testament's apocalyptic rendering of the future—and one which was permanently damaging on account of its combination with the Hellenistic spiritualization of the gospel—has been that the Hebraic sense of our responsibility towards those who will inherit *the earth*, our "children's children," was conspicuously diminished. Christians have been so busy preparing themselves and everybody else for heaven (or hell!) that they have regularly left the fate of earth, not to "the meek" to whom *Jesus* promises it, but to the ravenous, the power-hungry, the plunderers and grabbers! If it is the "Christian" West that has produced a technological society that persons of principle must describe as "leaderless," that eventuality ought to make us ponder some of the deficiencies of our avowed Christianity! Such pondering would no doubt bring us back again to the *basic* issue treated in the last chapter: whether *this world* does or does not matter to us, *as Christians*.

If it matters, then its *future* matters. That follows not only logically, as it would under any kinds of social circumstances, but today it follows as a matter of grave critical concern; for precisely the *future* of the world is at stake. Our immediate predecessors, at least our First World predecessors, took the future more or less for granted—the world's future, I mean. They assumed it would go on and on, and indeed that it would "get better and better." In Victorian England it was possible to lease a box in the Albert Hall for 999 years, "and many citizens did so."[13] How different it is now, less than a hundred years later! The future is no longer "assured" (a favorite word of all the Moderns); on the contrary it is all but assumed that what future we have before us will be fraught with ever-increasing hazards (famine, a poisoned environment, a burdensome population, war leading to nuclear armageddons—to mention only the *physical* hazards), and that "it can't go on." More and more frequently one hears older people commenting to the effect that they are glad they won't be around to face the music! (Compare this with Israel's patriarchs, who were always looking off into the far distant future when their children would be "more in number than the stars of the heavens or the sands of the earth"!) We seem to be capable of entertaining the idea of the Future only by cultivating a sort of programmed indifference to it, or feverishly trying to immerse ourselves wholly in the present, living it up—as those mortals have always done who sensed that "Tomorrow we die"!

Yet this is not only to present our world more and more unconditionally to the demonic forces that will in fact destroy it; it is also to destroy ourselves in the act of making ourselves indifferent to the future. For, as Dorothee Solle has put it succinctly, to be human is to have "an elemental relation to the future."[14] It is no more possible to live *only* in the present than it is to live *only* in the past. Physically and spiritually we are creatures who know ourselves to be moving from a past to a future; and the momentary, unmeasurable thing that we call the Present is comprised of nothing else except remembrance and hope. Moreover, as Paul Ricoeur has rightly said, in the last analysis remembrance and hope are "the same thing." How pathetic we are, then, when we try to live wholly in the present, without thinking of the future. Perhaps the "hollowness" (T.S. Eliot) of so much of contemporary life is to be traced to just this attempt. Having neither a past nor a future, and desiring nothing but the imagined pleasure of the present, we lack substance; we are human beings "without qualities" (Robert Musil).

To speak of stewardship today as implying a principle of futurization is to insist that as Christians it is our duty to *reclaim the future*. Not only our duty, but the duty of our species! Not as if it were simply ours to shape and possess. That is the boast of our Modern past, and it has brought us almost to ruin. The future is "in the hands of the Lord"—as the patriarchs also knew when they looked over the edge of Time into the generations of children yet unborn. They knew that they could not *control* the future, making it always safe and lovely and, naturally, "better"! They were not so foolish or so egotistical as to give themselves off as "masters of our fate." Trust, not certitude, was their stance vis à vis the future—trust in God, who is able to make even of our blundering work and plans something life-preserving. But working and planning we must nevertheless do, grocery store clerks though we be. For we are *stewards!* God has entrusted into our hands, as Pharoah entrusted to the prisoner Joseph, the future of the land. We know better than our forebears did how thoroughly inept we are for such a thing, even with all our machinery and Science and Think Tanks. (*Because of* all that, partly!) But if we could get over the dream of mastery (pride) and also over our disillusionment at finding ourselves no masters (sloth), we might be able to achieve certain "proximate goals" (Reinhold Niebuhr) that would at least ensure that our children's children would not inherit an ash-heap!

7 An Invitation

To conclude: I have used five rather awkward words to try, very superficially, to sketch the kind of spiritual, cultural, and physical revolution that could come to pass if once we began to permit the radical character of this ancient metaphor, reconsidered in the light of our own present "predicament" (Tillich) to invade our imaginations. We should, I have proposed, globalize, communalize, ecologize, politicize, and futurize this symbol that, for reasons of necessity but also as God's gift, has somehow been kept current in the vocabulary of our North American churches. The symbol itself will bear all these "enlarging" principles—easily! And the historical moment *demands* them.

But what if we really did such a thing? What if we allowed ourselves really to become open to the magnificent inclusiveness of this ancient symbol of our tradition? Well then, I suspect, we should find ourselves along with those in our churches who were troubled and inspired by this same consciousness, more and more at loggerheads with the dominant social forces of our society. For with every one of these five principles of expansion there is an implicit threat to the status quo:

- globalization can only occur against the entrenched spirit of narrow nationalism;
- communalization can take place only by confronting head on the persistent individualism of both society and religion;
- ecologization runs headlong into the spirit of technology and the mastery of nature;
- politicization along any lines but those of free enterprise immediately creates enemies in our society, and in our churches, too;
- futurization flies in the face of every private and institutional desire to have the good life here and now, to hell with our children's children!

In other words, a church that took stewardship seriously might well find itself in an ostracized, shut-out, countercultural situation—disestablished far beyond the mild limits it may have entertained for itself!

In other words, a church that took its stewardship of life quite literally might find itself amongst the poor more often than in the company of the rich; in the company of the protesting element more often than that of the powers that be; in the company of the oppressed more often than the oppressors.

In other words, a church that explored the depths of the stewardship vocation of Homo sapiens might have to suffer for its revolution.

In other words . . . a church!

VI STEWARDSHIP AND THE WORLDS

1 Our Problem

No discussion of The Problem of the Third World or The Problem of the Poor or the like should be trusted. Such titles betray a fundamental error in their authors' thought. The "problem of The Third World" is first the problem of *our* world, this so-called First World that is made up chiefly of the affluent nations of the North Atlantic. The poor are poor, and becoming yet poorer, because we are inordinately rich. It's our problem!

This does not mean that we are all equally rich. Nor does it mean that all our 'riches' is necessarily tainted and evil. There are certainly pockets of conspicuous poverty and oppression within our rich nations—a fact that is borne out by the aforementioned unemployment problem, and also by much of the racial and other unrest in our midst. As far as our wealth being tainted is concerned, it is surely quite legitimate if the average citizen of Canada, the U.S.A., France or Norway (e.g.) reminds the writers of such statements as I have just made that he/she only just manages, after all, to pay the monthly food bills, the rent or mortgage costs, educate the children, make payments on the car, and finance a modest vacation for the family. One can readily sympathize with the impatience and, occasionally, the anger of ordinary people in the First World when they are addressed as if they were directly to blame for the abject poverty of multitudes. Robert Hempfling speaks for many middle class church members when he writes: ". . . I'm tired of feeling guilty about being middle class and being characterized as mediocre, superficial, and banal in my thinking and lifestyle. I contend that such stereotyping is neither fair nor accurate."[1]

Obviously little is accomplished by the kind of "preaching" that engenders such reactions. It is no more effective for change, ultimately, than its medieval or puritan equivalent, the hell-fire-and-damnation sermon. We *are* guilty, and we need very desparately to be brought to a deep awareness of our guilt. But this cannot be achieved by laying guilt trips on individuals. The only sort of awareness of guilt that will lead to *metanoia* of a significant quality is one that comes through the patient and nonvindictive exposure of persons to the global realities that pertain in our larger context.

And, above all, this must lead to a consciousness of the *corporate* character of our guilt.

It is hard to understand corporate guilt when one's whole ethos is steeped in the myth of individualism. Although genuine *individuality* is one of the most difficult paths to walk in our conformist, fad-ridden society, we are all plagued from our youth up by the disease of individua*lism*. As we have noted in the preceding chapter's discussion of the principle of communalization, it is very hard for most North Americans at the emotional level (if not also intellectually) to escape the tenacles of this ideological octopus. From the outset we are urged on all sides to develop our personalities; to achieve our personal potential; to stand on our own two feet, etc. If we succeed it is because we've personally made the effort. If we fail we have somehow brought it upon ourselves—underachieved! How, in such an environment, can 'persons' avoid 'taking it personally' if they are told (e.g. by some young activist minister) that they are consuming 40% of the world's resources though they represent only six percent of the human population of Earth?

The first step towards change may be the necessity of learning, as First World citizens and members of the great middle classes in particular, how to *think corporately*. The prophet Isaiah, in the presence of the transcendent God, cried:

> . . . I am a man of unclean lips,
> And I dwell in the midst of a people of unclean lips . . . (Is. 6:5)

In order to achieve the right sort of awareness of *our* sin, we shall probably have to learn to reverse the order: (a) I dwell in the midst of a people of unclean lips; (b) I am a man/woman of unclean lips.

For that is in fact the order of things. We are guilty; each one of us is guilty; but the whole character of the sinful state of our world is distorted if we regard it in a simplistic way as if it were our individual sin—or even the sum total of our First World *personal* sins! Corporate sin and guilt is much more complicated than that. It has a different genesis and a different structure. Corporate sin and guilt has so to speak 'a life of its own'—as St. Paul knew when he said that we are not wrestling with flesh and blood but with "principalities and powers." Corporate sin would not be conquered even if, through personal guilt trips and the like, the majority of us managed somehow to slough off our personal greed, etc. In saying this, I have no intention of letting individuals (myself included!) off the hook. But we shall never rightly comprehend our personal involvement in evil until we begin to sense something of the immense dimensions of that corporate sin that our personal lives reflect, express and embody, but do not all by themselves create. The first principle of Sin, at least in today's world, is its corporateness: "I dwell in the midst of a people of unclean lips."

The problem of 'The Poor,' to come to the issue at hand, is our corporate problem—we who, taken together as a "people," must certainly in relation to them be named "the Rich." They (the Poor) are not without sin of course! They too have responsibilities and possibilities, corporately and personally, that they have neglected. "*All* have sinned and fallen short of the glory of God!". All! The Poor and the Rich alike. Later we shall try to reflect briefly on *their* problem, the problem of the poor, "underdeveloped" and "undeveloped" peoples of Earth. But since we *are* their problem at the level of its "efficient cause," we must begin there—with ourselves, corporately, as Problem. Until we comprehend that a little, even our half-hearted efforts to solve *their* problems will only complicate them further. As Jürgen Moltmann put it recently:

> The question is not what we can give them, but whether and when we are going to stop taking things from them. The poor nations are not our 'problem'. It is we—the rich, industrial nations—who are *their* problem.[2]

(a) Item: "North Americans throw away enough solid waste *each year* to build a wall 75 feet wide and 200 feet high along the Canada-U.S. border."[3]

Such a statistic raises innumerable questions. Perhaps if it were deeply probed it would contain all the questions there are! But one of them will suffice for now: By what spiritual forces must a society be driven if it amasses such a quantity of waste? Whole populations could, if they had access to such waste, survive on it! What impells a people that must cast away once-used bottles, tins, cartons; half-eaten steaks, fruit, vegetables; packaging that was unnecessary in the first place; cars that had lost their fashionable lines or a few spare parts; furniture, appliances, toys, machinery, etc., that had become outmoded, soiled, less convenient, less efficient, etc.? Is it simply *personal* ambition, greed, boredom . . . ?

A considerable part of the answer is implied in the following statement:

(b) Item: "In 1974, advertising in Canada cost about $1.4 billion, a per capita expenditure of about $64. This is about equal to the total federal and provincial government expenditures on medical, hospital and health services combined."[4]

The 'needs' of a society that wastes so much of its (earth's!) resources are only comprehensible if one understands that a very high proportion of those needs are artificially created by competitive agencies that have vested interests in making desires appear veritable requirements of daily existence. Even persons from the relatively well-off countries of the Second World, taken into a department or grocery store in North America or Western Europe, would be overwhelmed by the quantity and variety of goods available. For Third World citizens such stores are beyond the reach of earthly imagination. But we may ask: Is it really *necessary* that there should be 250 varieties of breakfast cereals in one place at one time?

Every year druggists must throw out large quantities of unpurchased prescription medicines whose expiry date has been reached. For this reason, the medicines must be sold at prices far exceeding their inherent worth. The reason: competing drug manufacturers produce variations of the same basic medicine and, since most medical practitioners prescribe by brand names, the druggists must stock all available brands. To pay for one sale, these businesses must include in its price all the items that will not be sold. Who is responsible? The doctors? The druggists? The manufacturers? The purchasers? The advertisers? Yes—all! And with some imagination this kind of absurdity can be challenged and changed![5] But one fears it will not be altered on a grand scale until it has been called into question by events that are terrible to contemplate. For it is an entrenched system, and so long as it serves the 'needs' of our people the majority seem oblivious to the fact that the famous "invisible Hand" that is supposed to be regulating this system must be busy most of the time collecting and disposing of garbage!

Such oblivion can be analyzed at many levels. At the most obvious level, it is a matter of our sheer ignorance. Most people appear to give little thought to the car graveyards they pass on the way to work or the insulting and infantile TV advertisements that entice them to get new cars. They are even less aware of the condition of the overwhelming majority of earth's human citizens, who cannot even count on *basic* needs being met, such as fresh water, let alone entertain in their mind's eye hundreds of varieties of soft and hard drinks! "In the 38 lowest income countries, only 28% of the population on the average have access to safe water, according to World Bank estimates (1980); the number of countries that have not yet been able to reach 50% of the population with safe water is well over 55, and may exceed 75. The rest of the people depend for their water on lakes, rivers, streams, irrigation canals, stagnant ponds and hand-dug wells—generally contaminated and often at great distances from home."[6] The *real* needs of the world's poor beggars the imagination even of our well-educated and informed citizenry:

(c) Item: "The misery of 2.5 billion persons is beyond the comprehension of the average American." In his book, *The Great Ascent*, Robert L. Heilbroner wrote a dramatic passage telling what would happen to an American family if its living standard were to be reduced to that of the underprivileged people of the world:

> 'We begin by invading the house to strip it of its furniture. Everything goes: bed, chairs, tables, television set. We will leave the family with a few old blankets, a kitchen table, a wooden chair . . . The box of matches may stay, a small bag of flour, some sugar and salt. A few

moldy potatoes already in the garbage can be rescued, for they will provide much of tonight's meal.

'The bathroom is dismantled, the running water shut off, the electric wires taken out. Next, we take away the house. The family can move to the toolshed. Communications must go next. No more newspapers, magazines, books . . . . Next, government services must go. No more postmen, no more firemen. There is a school but it is three miles away and consists of two rooms. They are not too overcrowded since only half the children in the neighborhood go to school.

'The nearest clinic is ten miles away and is tended by a midwife. It can be reached by bicycle provided the family has a bicycle, which is unlikely . . . Finally, money. We will allow our family a cash hoard of $5. . . . '[7]

While ordinary ignorance and incomprehension partly account for our indifference to the realities of our own overabundance as well as the destitution of the many, it is naive to think that this is a sufficient explanation. There are strong vested interests in our society that are served by this ignorance; they are by no means ready to excite or alarm the populace through programs of education and information that could in some degree combat this ignorance. We North Americans like to pride ourselves on being an open society, where news is not manipulated and information is available to all. It is true that in certain areas of information we are very open—sometimes to our detriment! But as one who has lived for significant periods in Europe—and in nations reputed to be highly circumspect and even secretive—I am convinced that the European public on the whole is *very* much better informed about the real character of the world we live in. I am also convinced that part of the reason for this (a rather significant part!) is that the primary medium of public information in major European countries (to wit, television) is not manipulated by private enterprise. There are, to be sure, a few provocative and critically informative programs on American and Canadian television networks; but what is with us the exception is more nearly the norm in West Germany, France, and England. Companies that want you to buy their gasoline and oil may be very happy to bring you entertaining family programs (or even opera!); but they are not likely to treat you to documentaries on the condition of peoples whose economies are in ruins partly on account of our inordinate consumption of the world's energy supplies. Or if they do so, it will be laced with the rhetoric of the "trickle-down theory," i.e. that the way to *world* prosperity is through greater prosperity in the "developed" nations.

The pathology of oblivion in the rich nations is not, however, exhausted by economic and political analysis, important as such analysis is. We have invoked the biblical doctrine of sin in the foregoing pages, and while the Bible knows perfectly well about the greed of capitalists who are ready to sell the widow and the orphan for a pair of shoes, it also knows that the corporate structures of sin and guilt are more subtle than the scheming of capitalists and entrepreneurs. The sinful consciousness (for example as it is so profoundly depicted in Genesis 3) expresses itself first and most characteristically in a falsification of reality. It hides and it lies. It is not for nothing that Jesus calls Satan "the Father of Lies"! The hiding and the lying that is the hallmark of sin should not be interpreted after the fashion of the petty moralists. "Thou shalt not lie," does not refer simplistically to telling fibs or making up explanations. It means the habit of constructing images of the world—world-views, ideologies, *imago homini*, etc.—that skillfully omit whole segments of experience and substitute theory for reality. The lying and hiding which belong to the sinful state makes much use of that psychic mechanism that Freud named repression: raw experience, including thought, is suspended at the subconscious level, blocked altogether, or transformed, before it is permitted to reach the level of conscious knowledge.

And now let us remember: We are not speaking just now only or simply of individual sin, but of corporate sin. When it is said (as many of the world's own wise have been saying now for a couple of decades) that ours is "a repressive society," that is what we should hear. Namely, that our corporate sin expresses itself most profoundly, not in the fact that our various authority structures suppress or manipulate the truth, but that we ourselves as a whole society are caught up in a *system of repression*. It is a *system*: that is, it transcends our individual wills; it is built into our institutions (education included); it is part of our total environment; it is 'natural.' To oppose or resist it is to swim against the stream, to do the 'unnatural' thing, and to be branded unnatural or devious or simply crazy as a consequence of it. Few therefore are driven to buck the system—and all the more so because those who do *not* buck it, but accept it, accept or promote it, are usually served very well by their comformity. But, as Ernest Becker put it bluntly, "Somebody has to pay for it." For his services, the Father of Lies asks a very high price: souls. But he takes his toll in bodies too. Those who pay bodily for the spiritual repression of the Rich nations are (who else?): the Poor.

"I dwell in the midst of a people of unclean lips."

I—the average person, am caught up in structures of deceit that automatically necessitate the suffering of others. But I find in myself neither the wisdom, the will, nor the courage to resist these structures. I am their victim, yet I am also (I know it!) served by them. So, yes, "I am a man, a woman of unclean lips."

(d) Item: ". . . we have to ask who this average man is. He may avoid the psychiatric clinic, but somebody around has to pay for it. We are reminded of those Roman portrait-busts that stuff our museums: to live in this tight-lipped style as an average good citizen must have created some daily hell. Of course we are not talking only about daily pettiness and the small sadisms that are practiced on family and friends. Even if the average man lives in a kind of obliviousness of anxiety, it is because he has erected a massive wall of repression to hide the problem of life and death. His anality may protect him, but all through history it is the 'normal, average men' who, like locusts, have laid waste to the world in order to forget themselves."[8]

The great weakness of repression as a defense mechanism against reality is that it is effective only up to a point: *viz* the point where the repressed truth asserts itself forcefully and refuses to be silenced or metamorphized by theory. (As I have sometimes put it, it was one thing for the "old lady" to "swallow a fly" and not notice it much; but when it came to the horse, truth had to assert itself, "Of course!") The rich nations have been remarkably adept at the repression of their own evil and the plight of their victims. This has worked, after a fashion, so long as the victims have been willing to endure the status quo and so long as the earth has been able to sustain our own rich expectations of it. But the victims have grown restive and conscious of their oppressed state (largely in direct proportion to the degree of their victimization), and the earth groans ever more perceptibly under the curse of a burgeoning population that makes ever more absurd demands upon its limited bounty. What our grandparents in North America were still able to repress, our grandchildren (perhaps our children) will have to face in the most open, ghastly and perhaps tragic way!

Because this is already known (but known without the repentance that accompanies the true knowledge of sin), the trend of the affluent on both sides of the ideological Curtain dividing First and Second Worlds is to prepare mightily for the defense of their systems:

(e) Item: " '. . . the cost of a ten-year programme to provide the essential food and health needs in developing countries is less than half of one year's military spending.' " (Taken from the Brandt Commission Report, 1980)

"The worldwide expenditure for military hardware has already surpassed US$ 450 billion annually, while official development aid remains below US$ 30 billion each year.

"The cost of one jet fighter plane could set up 40,000 village pharmacies."[9]

Ostensibly and on the surface of it, the incredible build-up of arms in the world is a matter between the First and Second Worlds, notably the USA and the USSR. But if one asks who is being *excluded*, both by the economic greed and the military hardware protecting that greed, one comes face-to-face with a deeper truth: Neither of those affluent worlds is prepared to lower its expectations so that the majority of Earth can be brought to more humane levels of existence. The noise and the drama of saber rattling between the two rich worlds ought not to distract our attention from the stealthy dealings both of them are performing with their left arms in the Third World. Let us not mistake it: the hardware is there *primarily* to protect the 'haves,' *whoever* they are and by whatever pompous theories they repress the truth, from the hungry, angry 'have-nots.'

2 Their Problem

Their problem, to speak now of the fact rather than its efficient cause, is simply their poverty. Only poverty is never simple. It is a complex amalgam of physical and spiritual pain, which robs the person and the community of dignity and meaning as much as it deprives the body of nourishment, shelter, and beauty.

> The starting point of all our considerations is poverty , or rather a degree of poverty which means misery, and degrades and stultifies the human person.[10]

It is of course oversimple to speak of The Third World as if we were treating a socio-geographic monolith. Poverty of the most abysmal type—the kind of poverty that cannot even be imagined by us, not even by most of the oppressed ones in our own midst—is to be found in what some are calling (to distinguish it from the less destitute) 'The Fourth World.' This term refers to almost one-fourth of the Earth's human population:

> The latest estimates indicate that some 800 million people in the world are destitute and live in conditions of absolute poverty. Their lives are characterized by malnutrition, under-nutrition, disease, illiteracy, unemployment, low income, inadequate shelter and high fertility. Some 40% of the population of the developing countries fall into this category, and most of these are found in rural sectors. . . .[11]

Those areas of the Third World not in such an abject state of poverty run the gamut from 'underdevelopment' to 'semi-development.' But just at this point we encounter the more subtle side of "their" problem. It is suggested both by the nomenclature of 'development' and by the fact that 'development' (i.e. the established models of life in the rich countries) is seen by the poor as well as most of their Western advisers as the solution of their problem. In other words, the problem of the poor nations is not only a poverty that is caused or sustained by our prosperity but a mentality that encourages them to want to *emulate* us. Thus, as William Ophuls points out, 'semi-developed' nations like Mexico and Brazil . . .

> . . . have followed a basically American path, so that Mexico City has a smog problem rivaling that of Los Angeles, and Brazil's treatment of its undeveloped wealth, especially such fragile and irreplaceable

resources as the Amazon rain forest, epitomizes frontier economics at its most heedless. On the other hand, Taiwan and South Korea have proceeded more or less along the lines laid down by Japan and are beginning to encounter many of the same problems. In the same way, the countries (now mostly beyond the stage of semi-development) that have travelled the Soviet path experience the same kinds of environmental problems and suffer from similar political liabilities in coping with them.[12]

It is understandable that human communities that are poor should look upon the rich peoples whose life their raw materials enhance, whose music and machinery they admire from afar, and whose well-dressed and over-fed tourists they encounter, as models to be imitated. What is less understandable is that the rich nations themselves should have produced so little depth of self-knowledge that their "Third World Experts" could assume the same sentiment! But this has in fact been the case:

> The ruling philosophy of development over the last twenty years has been: 'What is best for the rich must be best for the poor.' This belief has been carried to truly astonishing lengths, as can be seen by inspecting the list of developing countries in which the Americans and their allies and in some cases the Russians have found it necessary and wise to establish 'peaceful' nuclear reactors—Taiwan, South Korea, Phillipines, Vietnam, Thailand, Indonesia, Iran, Turkey, Portugal, Venezuela—all of them countries where overwhelming problems are agricultural and the rejeuvenation of rural life, since the great majority of their poverty-stricken peoples live in rural areas.[13]

The question that this 'problem of the worlds' poses for all of us, then, is a multidimensional one. It cannot be answered wisely simply by saying: "Bring them up to our standards," "Let them too become developed!", because the best minds amongst us know perfectly well not only that the Earth cannot sustain even its present population if all its peoples began to try to live as we do[14]; more than that, such wisdom is well aware that our vaunted development is scarcely a way of life guaranteed to bring abundance, let alone happiness. At the *Kirchentag* in Dusseldorf in 1973, some delegates were wearing tags that read: *"Hilfe! Wir sind entwickelt!"* (Help! We are developed!) Can anyone really believe that a world filled with our First World kind of living would be the best of all possible worlds? How does Christian stewardship speak to this 'problem of the worlds'?

3 Stewardship in the Global Village

(a) "The Earth IS the Lord's"

The first and most obvious point that must be made out of the faith in which we stand is that the primary object of Christian efforts at effecting change must be our own society. It is we, not the masses of the poor, who are judged by the 'theo-anthropology' of stewardship. This does not preclude the necessity of other types of activity in relation to the poor, including direct aid. But one can only be pessimistic about the long-range results of aid programs unless they are accompanied by a massive self-examination on the part of the givers.

If we are at all serious about stewardship as a symbol of Christian and human existence, then the thing that has to come under direct attack in our prophetic witness within our own First World is the whole notion of mastery and ownership inherent in our world view. For North Americans in particular, the questioning of the right to possess and to dispose of one's possessions in whatever way one chooses appears almost an act of treason! Somehow the ideas of possession and mastery took root in our soil more tenaciously than elsewhere—perhaps because so many of our forebears had themselves been have-nots. And having had the benefits of rich natural resources, in whose bounty large numbers of people could have some share, we have grown accustomed to thinking of ourselves chiefly as possessors (Consider the expression: "So-and-so is *worth* such-and-such an amount of money.") 'Having' seems a veritable "human right" with us: having property, having material goods, having houses and cars and every imaginable appliance; having, also, less tangible things—health, the confidence of the well-fed, power over others, etc. Moreover the churches have never seriously challenged this kind of thinking; their periodic outbursts over "materialism" have all the signs of ritual corporate flagellation, easing the guilty conscience. On the contrary, our religion has undergirded and legitimized our acquisitiveness, and most of our churches reflect in their own physical manifestations (church buildings and properties) the same propensity to judge worth by possessions as is found in our homes, schools, and places of work. The truncated nature of stewardship in our Christian practice shows up nowhere more conspicuously than in the budgets of churches, which regularly demonstrate the *self*-serving priorities of local congregations.

If however we take even with a modicum of seriousness the criticism of the whole idea of possession that is built into the steward symbol biblically conceived, then we must begin to register a prophetic critique of the institution of property. I do not mean that such a critique ought to be carried to the absurd lengths of doctrinaire and utopian communism—that is the quickest way to render it ridiculous and untenable. Obviously there is that in the human spirit (whether it belongs to creation or fall is hard to say!) that craves ownership. Of something or other, even if it is only a token, I need to be able to say: "This is mine." But there is a difference, surely, between the need to say that about a few books and pictures and perhaps even a house and, on the other hand, thousands of acres of land or mineral rights of a whole area or dozens of houses in the slums of big cities. The symbolic necessity of having something that is "mine"—something that will give me a sense of continuity with my own past, for example—is not going to be taken from me if I am denied the right to own three city blocks! The Hebraic side of our faith never questioned the first kind of ownership, because it knew (and still knows) that as physical beings we need to express our spiritual yearnings and joys physically. But the Hebraic prophets certainly did rail out against the rich who found their spiritual "worth" in their riches and—as is usual—through regarding the lives of their fellow human beings as worth-less. If we may borrow a leaf from the Marxist notebook, we may say as Christians, surely, that there is a point where a change in *quantity* introduces a *qualitative* change (Lenin's Law). Given certain needs and obligations, it may be perfectly necessary for Smith to maintain a bank account in six figures. But when Smith's account grows to seven figures, watch out! Something will probably have happened to Smith, and it will not just be the effects of inflation! From being a man who kept up his bank account for utilitarian reasons, our friend Smith has likely become one whose bank account is of special interest to him in its own right—and therefore a symbol of a very different nature from the one about which we have been thinking just now: the symbol of power, self-sufficiency, "worth"; the same symbol as the one represented by those "greater barns" Jesus's "rich fool" considered erecting just the night he was called to give an account of his stewardship!

"The earth is *the Lord's* and the fulness thereof . . ." Possession is an illusion at best—a pathetic quest for significance more often.

Bringing this down to the concretes of our present situation, It means that the Christian community, to be true to its own roots, will increasingly have to be found on the side of those who argue that the basic resources of the earth *belong* neither to individuals, nor companies, nor nations, but are global treasures, given by a gracious God to "all the families of the earth"—including those not yet born. The preservation and distribution of these treasures must not be allowed therefore to fall into the hands of a few who, through such control, ensure their own brief moment of prosperity at the expense of the survival and welfare of earth's creatures for generations to come. The globalization principle applies here, as does futurization, communalization, politicization, and ecologization. If we have made these principles our own, having first made sure that as Christians this world really is our business, then we are led to very explicit conclusions such as this one about the institution of property in the context of the global village.

Let us be honest: this probably means that an obedient Christian community today will find itself in the company of groups and persons whose ideas are presently highly suspect so far as the dominant culture of the First World is concerned. For both the economics of capitalism and the sociology of nationalism must be questioned by a stewardship theology that reckons (as we must) globally. (The recent criticism of the World Council of Churches is a small indication of the wrath that may yet come!) I repeat: this does not imply that Christians must embrace either an ideological socialism or the sort of transcendent internationalism that has no room for the love of 'one's own.' The collective greed of international communism is no answer to the competitive individualistic greed of capitalism. But I do not see how a *serious* stewardship today can avoid seeking more just forms for the preservation and distribution of earth's wealth, for a more truly global expression of the love of God for earth's creatures, and for a future that lasts well beyond the next election year!

(b) "He Hath Filled the Hungry . . ."

Obviously the work of transforming an acquisitive and imperialistic society into one that is capable of proximate forms of economic justice is a *long-range* goal of Christian stewardship. But to all who continue to jibe at the idealism of such a goal let it be said that the future is on the side of this ideal and against all the practical people! It is no longer either practical or practicable to assume that such grossly unequal distribution of the planet's resources can continue to be the norm. The First World will either *learn* some measure of sharing or it will be *taught*—and the lessons will not be gentle ones. We ought to know after some centuries of observing the laws of "competition" that those who play that game are "First" only temporarily!

But in the meantime the plight of the poor cannot wait for the transformation of the rich. The second strategy of Christian stewardship must therefore be the steward's care of earth's greatest victims. There is never any excuse for leaving the one who has fallen amongst thieves lying in the ditch to die—not even the excuse of converting the thieves! Aid must be given, and it must be given regardless of the identity, color, political persuasion, etc. of the victims. The aid must be appropriate to the need: it is the victim who determines what need means. If the victim says "I am hungry," it is not for the steward to determine, sophist-like, that this of course means spiritual hunger and proceed to offer the gospel for balm. I shall reserve until the last chapter my answer to those who are afraid that when the church gets involved in the provision of material aid it will forget its spiritual Mission. In his parable defining both the neighbor and our obedience in relation to the neighbor, Jesus at no point commanded his followers to use the occasion of the other's physical need to engage in a program of Christian indoctrination! Not even when the Samaritan took his leave of the victim, whose life was now out of danger and who was presumably rather comfortably set up in the inn—not even then did the Samaritan exact spiritual payment from the victim by making him listen to a sermon. He didn't even leave a tract, discretely, with the innkeeper, to be given to the patient when he was a little stronger. At least with the 25 percent of the world's poor who are *desperately* poor, *direct assistance* must be given—without strings!

Direct assistance is certainly no profound answer to the problem of "the worlds," and it can offer interim relief only for "their" part of the problem. But of course it must be given, and in far greater quantities and much greater openness to the needs of the victims than is presently the case. Persons and nations who do not act out of Christian motivation may think otherwise; but at least for Christians the thing has been decided already: Christian stewardship *means* feeding the hungry with good things.

(c) The Stewardship of Experience

Without in any way minimizing the importance of such aid, however, it must be adjudged little more than Band Aid treatment without the stewardship revolution applied at home, and without sharing something else that in the long-run is more important than bread. Here I should like to combine my own thought with that of a Christian thinker for whom I have the greatest respect, and who in my opinion has shown us the way of Christian stewardship as it applies to "the rich" in a manner more imaginative and more practical than almost anyone I can think of: E.F. Schumacher.

It is Schumacher's conviction that what bedevils our approach to the Third World is our assumption that they should emulate us: "What is good for the rich is good for the poor." This, he says, is the thinking of people (economists and others) who think about problems, and populations, and Gross National Products, but not about *people*. Who are *the people* who constitute the Third World? Answer: They are poor people! They are the people (as he says in the title of a chapter of "Two Million Villages." So . . .

> The new thinking that is required for aid and development will be different from the old because it will take poverty seriously. It will not go on mechanically, saying, 'What is good for the rich must also be good for the poor.' It will care for people—from a severely practical point of view. Why care for people? Because people are the primary and ultimate source of any wealth whatsoever. If they are left out, if they are pushed around by self-styled experts and high-handed planners, then nothing can ever yield real fruit.[15]

If development means developing the potentiality of the human beings who constitute the have-not nations, then the *primary* emphasis must be—not upon goods, but upon the "education, organization, and discipline" of the people:

> Without these three, all resources remain latent, untapped, potential. There are prosperous societies with but the scantiest basis of natural wealth, and we have had plenty of opportunity to observe the primacy of invisible factors after the war. Every country, no matter how devastated, which had a high level of education, organization, and discipline produced an 'economic miracle.' In fact these were miracles only for people whose attention was focused on the tip of the iceberg. The tip had been mashed to pieces, but the base, which is education, organization and discipline, was still there.[16]

Development in this sense cannot be created by feeding a society better food or providing it with nuclear reactors! Such development "requires a process of education." But this does not mean that it requires *centuries*—centuries we do not have! In the course of their own, slow evolution, the peoples of the West have learned some things that can be passed on rather quickly—*provided* it is remembered that these lessons are to be geared to the real situation of *the people*, and not simply to satisfy the theoretical presuppositions of the modern Western mind concerning what makes for The Good Life.

Just this is where I should like to supplement Schumacher's admirable program. For very understandable reasons, he concentrates on the positive side of what we First World people could pass on to our sisters and brothers of the Third World. In a word, it is the kind of practical know-how that can assist poor people in "two million villages" to develop the "intermediate technology" ("small" or "appropriate" technology) that would enable them to live with relative prosperity and dignity *in* their villages, instead of taking their poverty from the village to the city (as they do now), where it becomes even more horrendous. As Schumacher puts it:

> Give a man a fish . . . and you are helping him a little bit for a short while; teach him the art of fishing and he can help himself all his life. On a higher level: supply him with fishing tackle; this will cost you a good deal of money, and the result remains doubtful; but even if fruitful, the man's continuing livelihood will still be dependent on you for replacements. But teach him how to make his own fishing tackle and you have helped him to become not only self-supporting but also self-reliant and independent.[17]

The logic of this, and of the whole approach of intermediate technology, seems to me above reproach. But there is one condition that I think he has not adequately met: he has neglected the fact that for First World citizens, experts or otherwise, to transmit such knowledge, they must themselves have come to a high degree of *self*-knowledge concerning the limitations, dangers, and undesirable effects of their own high technocracies. *And* they must be able imaginatively and passionately to transmit *that* knowledge to the

Third World, whose peoples naturally suppose that big technology alone brings human beings success, and who are very apt to suspect First World citizens who would withhold the great blessings of technocracy of wanting to hoard those blessings for themselves. I am in total agreement with Schumacher that "The best aid to give is intellectual aid, a gift of useful knowledge."[18] But a very significant part of that knowledge must be the knowledge of *ourselves* as a less than happy, less than egalitarian, less than free, and perhaps even as a doomed civilization! This is the negative (but is it really negative?) lesson that must accompany our positive gifts of know-how, if the latter are to be in any sense of the words honest, authentic, sincere. For the problem of the Third World, as we have said, is not only that it does not have, but that it is driven by unseen forces to imitate those who do have—who may indeed have "gained the whole world" and lost their soul. Along with our *knowledge*, in other words, we might be able on the basis of our unique experience of "the technological society" to share some *wisdom*.

VII STEWARDSHIP AS KEY TO A THEOLOGY OF NATURE

1 Christian Culpability

"Nature is the enemy! She must be brought to her knees!" Such were the triumphant words of the narrator of an unforgettable documentary film that I saw some decade or so ago. The screen pictures to which these words gave expression as a kind of litany showed us a vast upheaval, an explosion caused (one supposes) by tons of dynamite: rocks and trees and water and (in all likelihood) several thousands of little animals went rushing pell-mell heavenwards. And when the dust settled there were the earth movers and the heavy machinery, ready to turn the wilderness of the north into one of the great hydroelectric projects of our continent. This undertaking, the actual need and worth of which has been seriously challenged by many scientists, economists, and politicians, is a monument to the technocratic mentality.

But what was so vexing to me as I viewed this film was that the same script, in which "Nature" was identified as "the Enemy," was studded with quotations from the Bible. I don't remember all of them, but some of the following were certainly used:

> And God . . . said to them, "Be fruitful and multiply, and fill the earth and subdue it; and have dominion over the fish of the sea and over the birds of the air and over every living thing that moves upon the earth." (Genesis 1)

> And God blessed Noah and his sons, and said to them, "Be fruitful and multiply, and fill the earth. The fear of you and the dread of you shall be upon every beast of the earth, and upon every bird of the air, upon everything that creeps upon the ground and all the fish of the sea; into your hands they are delivered. Every moving thing that lives shall be food for you . . . . I give you everything. (Genesis 9)

> . . . what is man that thou art mindful of him . . .
> Yet thou hast made him little less than God,
>   and dost crown him with glory and honour.
> Thou hast given him dominion over the works
>   of thy hands,
> Thou hast put all things under his feet, (Psalm 8)
> 'Look at the birds of the air . . . . Are you not of more value than they?' (Matthew 6)

> But these, like irrational animals, creatures of instinct, born to be caught and killed . . . will be destroyed in the same destruction with them . . . (II Peter 2)

A year or so later, when my friends in the life sciences at the University of Saskatchewan began to demand of me why we Christians had such a deplorable view of nature, I understood something of what they meant. They showed me the then newly-published essay of the historian Lynn White, Jr.: "The Historical Roots of our Ecologic Crisis."[1] Professor White's article, which has since become a kind of encyclical amongst the friends of nature and has been reprinted in many places, makes a clear-cut case: Behind the modern pillage of planet Earth there stands the Hebraic-Christian religion with its too lofty estimate of the human species, its frank denigration of the animal and vegetable kingdoms, and its insistence that humanity has both the right and the duty to rule. Have dominion! Subdue! The two words (as Loren Wilkinson reminds us in a recent article for *Christianity Today*) are in Hebrew very strong ones: *Kabash* (subdue) "comes from a Hebrew root meaning to tread down; it conveys the image of a heavy-footed man making a path by smashing everything in his way." The connotation of *radah* (dominion), Wilkinson continues, "is no less harsh; it also conveys a picture of 'treading' or 'trampling' and suggests the image of a conqueror placing his foot on the neck of a slave."[2] Technology, wrote Lynn White, Jr.,

> . . . .is at least partly to be explained as an Occidental voluntarist realization of the Christian dogma of man's transcendence of, and rightful mastery over, nature . . . . Our science and technology have grown out of Christian attitudes towards man's relation to nature which are almost universally held not only by Christians and neo-Christians but also by those who fondly regard themselves as post-Christians.[3]

What are we to make of this? Is biblical faith especially culpable in connection with the industrial oppression of the natural world? How can we reconcile (or can we?) the apparent contradictions of a religion that on the one hand clearly makes "the world"—God's "good" creation—the very object of the divine agape, and on the other seems to give to greedy Anthropos all the justification he needs for turning the beautiful place God made into a pig sty?

One thing is certain: The technocratic approach to existence has evolved within a civilization whose most influential *religious* background has been one that called itself "Christian." It is in particular the humanity of our "Christian" West that Rachell Carson (perhaps the first person to draw contemporary attention to the rape of nature) had in mind when she wrote:

> I am pessimistic about the human race because it is too ingenious for its own good. Our approach to nature is to beat it into submission.

> We would stand a better chance of survival if we accommodated our-
> selves to this planet and viewed it appreciatively, instead of skepti-
> cally and dictatorially.[4]

Does beating nature into submission accurately express the meaning of "have dominion . . ."? Are skepticism and dictatorship
authentically *Christian* attitudes towards the planet? Or does Christianity somehow, even unwittingly, encourage such attitudes? How,
in the face of much ecological bitterness directed at the Judeao-
Christian worldview, can we describe the relation between
humanity and the rest of creation—if not to exonorate ourselves
from guilt, at least to contribute something better to the future?

In my response to these questions I shall consider three possible
(as well as actual and historical) ways of considering the relation
between humanity and nature: (1) Humanity Above Nature; (2)
Humanity In Nature; and (3) Humanity With Nature.

2 Humanity Above Nature

One way of conceiving of this relation is to place Homo sapiens
on a very high rung of the ladder of being, and to insist that nature is
simply there for human usage. At the outset of the Modern period,
Western philosophic literature was crammed full of this sentiment.
Indeed, the sentiment is of the essence of modernity! One of the
most straightforward statements of it comes from the pen of the
English philosopher Thomas Hobbes, who overagainst the Medieval propensity to regard nature cautiously, as a realm of immense
mystery, wrote:

> She is no mystery, for she worketh by motion and geometry . . . . [we]
> can chart these motions. Feel then as if you lived in a world which
> can be measured, weighed and mastered and confront it *with
> audacity*.[5]

Another man, René Descartes, who shaped our epoch, put the matter in somewhat gentler terms, but his claim for humanity is if anything even more extravagant than Hobbes':

> I perceived it to be possible to arrive at a knowledge highly useful in
> life, and in room of the speculative philosophy usually taught in the
> schools, to discover a practical [philosophy], by means of which,
> knowing the force and action of fire, water, the stars, the heavens
> and all other bodies that surround us, as distinctly as we know the
> various crafts of our artisans, we might also apply them in the same
> way to all the uses to which they are adapted, and thus render our-
> selves *lords and possessors of nature*.[6]

Maitre et possesseur de la nature! Francis Bacon reduced the sentiment to a slogan: *Scientia est potestas* (Science is power). We
achieve knowledge (scientia) of our world, not for the beauty of

knowing (that was the aim of the ancients—*sapientia*: wisdom), but for *power* (potestas).

This has been the dominant attitude of Modern Western civilization into our own time. You can hear it still, chanted on every television advertisement, inserted openly or implicitly into nearly every political speech, and—perhaps in its most characteristic form nowadays—in the grim declarations of the architects of warfare. "Science is power." "Modern technics," wrote Bertrand Russell in the late 'forties,

> . . . is giving man a sense of power which is changing his whole mentality. Until recently the physical environment was something that had to be accepted. But to the modern man the physical environment is merely the raw material for manipulation and opportunity. It may be that God made the world, but there is no reason why we should not make it over.[7]

It is interesting to note that the same Bertrand Russell, near the end of his long life, confided in a BBC radio interview that he was pessimistic whether we would see the end of the present century.

However we may feel personally about the Man Above Nature syndrome, we are part of a society that has been built upon that premise. The idea that humanity is nature's "lord and possessor," capable of making over what God rather thoughtlessly put together in the first place, is an almost exact description of the North American attitude towards the natural universe. It is our very birthright. We are, as George Grant has so ably stated it, the children of the Modern epoch; we have no other past than the Modern past:

> It is hard indeed to overrate the importance of faith in progress through technology to those brought up in the main stream of North American life. It is the very ground of their being. The loss of this faith for a North American is equivalent to the loss of himself and the knowledge of how to live. The ferocious events of the twentieth century may batter the outposts of that faith, dim intuitions of the eternal order may put some of its consequences into question, but its central core is not easily surrendered.[8]

It is ingrained in our most rudimentary thinking as a people that nature, which has been exceptionally bounteous in our case, is there for the taking, the making, the breaking. The ironical poem of Lewis Carol might have been written with North Americans in mind:

> The Walrus and the Carpenter
> Were walking close at hand;
> They wept like anything to see
> Such quantities of sand;
> If this were only swept away,
> They said, it would be grand.
> If seven maids with seven mops
> Swept it for half a year,

> Do you suppose, the Walrus said,
>   That they could get it clear?
> I doubt it, said the Carpenter,
>   And shed a bitter tear.

We have swept and mopped and cleared the natural world until it is hard to find any traces of it in our more urbanized areas. As Ogden Nash lamented,

> I think that I shall never see
> A billboard lovely as a tree;
> Indeed, unless the billboards fall,
> I'll never see a tree at all!

And there are still people in our urban jungles who 'shed bitter tears' because we cannot yet control quite everything. The weather still holds surprises—though the animal world is succumbing with alacrity to our designing instincts. The case of the turkey is symbolic:

> When Audubon painted it, it was a sleek, beautiful, though odd-headed bird, capable of flying 65 miles per hour. Benjamin Franklin said that it should be adopted as America's national bird, thinking it a 'more respectable bird' than the 'poor and often lousy' Bald Eagle. Today, the turkey is an obese, immobile thing, hardly able to stand, much less fly. As for respectability, the big bird is so stupid that it must be taught to eat, and so large in the breast that in order to breed, a saddle must be strapped to the hen to offer the turkey cock a claw-hold. The modern bird is not so much a turkey as it is a mutation, a commodity manufactured rather than a bird hatched. It has been forced to become a sort of feathered Jane Mansefield, sporting 60% of its flesh in the breast and wings. Americans like white meat, and the American poultry industry, using methods that may harm you, is happy to remodel its birds in order to comply.[9]

Is all of this really the product or by-product of the Judeao-Christian tradition? I doubt it. There are many things in the biblical tradition that go against the grain of such a manipulative approach to nature. Amongst them (a subject to which we will presently return) is the Bible's way of associating such manipulation, not with the positive will of God, but with *dis*obedience. Nature suffers, not when human beings are doing what they are intended to do, but when they *sin*. The following passage from Isaiah could be taken as a text for the sermons of the most ardent of nature's friends:

> The earth mourns and withers,
>   the world languishes and withers;
>   the heavens languish together with the earth.
> The earth lies polluted
>   under its inhabitants;
> for they have transgressed the laws,
>   violated the statutes,
>   broken the everlasting covenant.

Therefore a curse devours the earth,
  and its inhabitants suffer for their guilt;
therefore the inhabitants of the earth are scorched,
  and few men are left.
The wine mourns,
  the vine languishes,
  all the merry-hearted sigh . . .
The city of chaos is broken down,
  every house is shut up so that none can enter.
There is an outcry in the streets for lack of wine;
  all joy has reached its eventide;
  the gladness of the earth is banished.

(24:4 ff.)

But even on strictly historical grounds it is naive to trace the idea that humanity is above nature in such an unambiguous, undialectical way to the biblical tradition. If it were of the essence of our tradition, then why did not the early Christians and the imperial church of the Middle Ages already institute such a conception of the human species? Why did it have to wait for a thousand years and more for this allegedly Christian conception to flower? Leonardo de Vinci at the close of the Middle Ages already knew about the submarine; but he refused to pass along the idea to his aristocratic patrons, because he believed humanity too diabolical to have that secret. Like the Greeks of old, Medieval Christians were for *limiting* human power. They did not look upon scientia as *potestas* but as truth—*veritas*. They wanted wisdom, not mastery.

The real roots of our Humanity Above Nature complex are not in Christianity per se but in the admixture of Reformation (especially Reformed) Christianity and Renaissance Humanism that began to appear upon the European scene just about the time the man Columbus decided to master the Atlantic. (His decision was certainly inspired by the general atmosphere that we have been chronicaling here. His own character fits the new *imago* rather well. This "giant of a redhead, six feet tall at a time when the average virile male was about five feet four" was, as Alistair Cooke writes in his *America*, "a fast-talking, obsessive egomaniac who combined in curiosity, romantic stubbornness, and sense of mission something of a Galileo, Don Quixote, and John the Baptist." He was also "A Christian of almost maniacal devoutness [who] longed for the secular trappings of pomp and power, and, beginning with the Indies, he would convert every prince and pauper he encountered and have himself proclaimed governor of every land and island he discovered."[10]) As the Columbus character and deed indicate, the new conception of human nature and destiny that emerged from this meeting contained many elements of post-Constantinian Christianity. But it also left something out: the darker side of the Medieval analysis, which contained the insight that humanity's *use* of power is frequently directed towards evil ends; and the mysticism of the Middle Ages that had implications for its conception of the natural world.[11]

This, however, does not exonerate the Christian tradition—or rather, while it may in some sense exonerate Christianity or at least biblical religion, it does not exonerate the Christians! For one must ask: Why did the Christians at the turn of the Modern epoch and beyond permit Christianity to be used in this way? Why were they not more diligent (and why are *we* not?) in saying to the Bacons and Descartes and Eric Hoffers and B.F. Skinners of this world that the name our religious tradition has given to the human quest for power without love is *Sin*?

Instead, we have either aided and abetted the whole process of denigrating nature by openly supporting the Modern quest for mastery, or by indulging in the kinds of theological pronouncements and emphases that were naive about their context and therefore did not ask how such statements could be *used*. Perhaps the latter is the more characteristic reason for our lack of prophetic insight; for it is only rarely during the course of these two thousand years that Christianity has been critically aware of its context. For the most part, Christians (including Christian intellectuals) have pronounced Christian Truth with very little regard for the manner in which it could be heard and used. Thus, for example, much of the theology of the *imago Dei* concept ("so God created man in his own image") has readily supported an anthropology of Humanity Above Nature. The following statement is typical:

> Man is a creature divinely endowed with gifts which set him above all other creatures: he is made in the image of God.[12]

Had the theologians been more contextually attuned, they might have thought twice before making such pronouncements! Of course, they might also have learned from the Biblical *text* (quite apart from their context) that the image of God *does not refer to a quality that we possess*, making us so much better than the other creatures, but to a *relationship in which we stand* vis a vis our Creator. And this relationship does not set us "above all other creatures"; it makes us *responsible for* and *representative of* the others![13] As stewards of them, let us say!

3 Humanity In Nature

The second theoretical and historical possibility of conceiving of the relation between human beings and the natural world is to think of Homo sapiens as one of the myriad creatures, nothing more; one species among others, mortal as they, dependent as they, having no more to offer than they, and no more right to life either. Humanity *In* nature.

This conception of the place of the human species is also, so far as its historical application is concerned at any rate, a Modern one. It is possible to find hints of it here and there in earlier civilizations and religions. One can discover such hints also in the Scriptures of Israel and the church. Amongst these, none is more significant than that picture of *ha Adam* provided in the second (and oldest) of the two creation sagas of Genesis: *Adam* is taken from *Adamah*—or, as Loren Wilkinson translates the Hebrew pun, "God made humans out of humus."[14] In this connection, too, we could think of the many places in the Bible where the character and the destiny of the human creatures is compared to that of all the others—

> All flesh is grass,
>> and all its beauty is like the flower of the field.
> The grass withers, the flower fades,
>> when the breath of the Lord blows upon it;
>> surely the people is grass.
> The grass withers, the flower fades;
>> but the word of our God will stand forever.
>
> (Isaiah 40:6-8)

Yet in the literature of the Bible as in other ancient sources, humanity is hardly ever *just* grass. There is a mystery about this being—the mystery of mind, of *Geist* (ghost, spirit). This mystery prevents the ancients both of Jerusalem and of Athens from regarding *Anthropos* as "just another animal." To be sure, the creature is animal; but it is a thinking animal, a "rational animal" (Greece), a "speaking animal" (Jerusalem). Its thinking and speaking is not always good for it. Thinking does not make it happy most of the time. Evil flows from its tongue. And "no human being can tame the tongue—a restless evil, full of deadly poison" (James 3:9) and its imagination is perhaps evil altogether. Yet thought and the articulation of thought do render this creature somehow . . . transcendent. The ancients are nearly unanimous on this point, though they accentuate different things.

The tendency to "naturalize" humanity and to make a program of it belongs rather to our own historical epoch—as does the placing of humanity *above* nature. In fact, it is a clear *reaction* to the latter! It is the reaction of a protesting element against the spirit of the Enlightenment and the industrialization and technicization of existence that flowed from the Enlightenment mentality. It is the Romantic reaction. Against the elevation of the human species along the lines of an almost divine rationality, the Romantics rebelled on the side of "the heart," on the side of Nature. From Rousseau onwards, they fought against the Modern world's rationalistic reduction of humanity. For they saw (quite rightly) that this supposed elevation of the human species *above* nature was at the same time a denigration of the species. Turning humanity into nothing but brain could lead to a situation in which everything about

Homo sapiens that is *not* brain (feeling, love, emotion, the body, sex, tears, etc.) would have to be repressed or if possible dispensed with!

They did not err in their judgment. The technocrats are providing us with foolproof methods for dispensing with all the unpredictable, messy elements in the life of the human creature—freedom and dignity and the like! "Science is power" has, as we have seen, come to mean power over the human species too. What is going on with the turkeys is not just what is going on with the turkeys! (Is there any connection between this and the contemporary appellation of human beings as "turkeys"?) If you start out, as did Hobbes and Descartes and others, to dominate nature, you must come at last to the domination of human nature (the 'Catch 22' of the process). You cannot have a world that is fully controlled and "possessed" in the hands of creatures who themselves are not in command of their "lower parts," their emotions, their whims and moods, their physical drives, etc. The ironical thing about the idea of humanity being above nature is that it has to destroy all that is natural in human beings in order to work. So by now, as Heschel has reminded us, the efficient machine is a more acceptable model for humankind than is Aristotle's "rational *animal.*"

The "Romantic Rebellion" (Sir Kenneth Clark) was a necessary protest in behalf of what is "natural" in humanity against the industrial society's reduction of humanity to rationality. The need for this protest is by no means over.

But sometimes when the pendulum of history swings it goes too far. Extremes beget extremes, and we find ourselves caught between one absurd reduction and another. Thus in the past two or three decades, and in the face of a technocracy that has gone much farther than ever Bacon or Descartes intended, there has come to be in the Western world and especially in North America a movement that carries the idea of humanity being *in* nature to ridiculous conclusions. It is now possible to hear even Christians speaking as if the only way of saving the planet were for the human species to plan itself out of existence. To become as "natural" as the dinosaurs!

I shall never forget the first time I heard this sentiment expressed publicly. It was in the 1960's, when the deplorable state of the natural world had just come to everyone's attention; and this awareness begot an interdisciplinary course in our university that we called "Man and the Biosphere." (Everyone's attention had not yet caught onto sexist language!) During the first several weeks of this course, one academic discipline after another paraded before the large student assembly and told of the devastations wrought upon the natural world by technocratic "Man." Then one night there was a panel discussion, and from the student audience this question emerged. ("Emerged" is I think the right word. The young woman who articulated it did so slowly, as if she were making a discovery in the very act of pronouncing the words): "If Man is the *problem* of the Biosphere," she began, "wouldn't the world be . . . better off . . . without him?"

My scientific colleagues on the panel did not know what to make of that, so they turned spontaneously to me (I am proud to record that as the one defender of God in the teaching staff of the course I was also perceived as Man's defender—frequently "his" *only* defender, in fact!). Obviously someone had to answer, because the student's question was not just one student's question; it was *the* question, it hung in the atmosphere waiting to find an amanuensis, some Cassandra or other who would actually ask it! Every lecturer had begged it, and now it could no longer be avoided.

I do not now remember exactly what I said, but what I should like to think of myself as having said is something like this: "What would it mean, after the disappearance of the thinking animal *Anthropos*, to use a term like 'better off'? Would the elephants hold a congress and announce in position papers that now, certainly, the world was better off than during the reign of Homo sapiens? Would the cockroaches organize a service of worship, and would all the creatures be handed mimeographed copies of a newly composed *Te Deum*, 'Now O Lord of Hosts we are better off! Praise God for the death of his creature Adam, bless him O Ye stars and hails for Eve's demise . . .' "?

There is no doubt that the human species has created more trouble in the world than any other creature. Christians already affirmed this long ago when they made the "fall of creation" the consequence of Adam's fall. But is the healing of creation to be achieved through the *extinction* of the troublesome creature? Not as I read the story of our . . . redemption! Besides, Yahweh already thought of that solution—as the story of the great flood tells us, mythically. Is the only way of saving *the world*, then, to circumscribe and chain down and control the human creature—perform as it were some kind of super-lobotomy upon its brain so that it could do neither evil nor good, just *be*? Place it, so to speak, so unambiguously *in* nature that it could have no hand in the destroying *or* keeping *of* nature? Must the human priest be so totally defrocked?

That, it seems to me, is not only a counsel of despair but patent nonsense. Even the limiting of our powers—even the entire sacrifice of our powers!—presupposes that we are after all unique creatures, who do not *simply* do "what comes naturally."

4 Humanity With Nature

We are lead through these reflections to a third possible way of conceiving of the relation between humanity and the natural order. I suspect that it must be regarded more as *possibility* than as a way that has actually been given a chance in history. It has certainly been envisaged, however, even if it has not been consistently enacted. For it is without doubt the possibility that inheres in our Judeo-Christian tradition: Humanity *With* Nature. Not above it. Not merely in it. But with it.

Have you ever noticed the prominence in the Bible of the preposition, "with"? Husbands like Adam are said to be "with" their wives, and vice versa. Friends are with their friends—as Jesus's disciples were with him here, with him there. Even God himself is described in these terms: *Emmanuel*, "God with us."

This has to be so, of course, because the *language* of the Scriptures is controlled by its ontology, its view of reality; and in the biblical ontology everything is both identified with everything else and different from everything else. Peter is a human being like John, but he is not just a carbon copy of John. And Eve is not Adam—does not belong to Adam, even if she is "bone of his bones, flesh of his flesh." The animals in Genesis II are made out of the same dust as the "earth-creature" (Trible) Adam, but they differ from Adam too, and will not do as his partner. The creation as a whole is different from its Creator—it is certainly not just an emanation, as in other religions; it is *very* different, *totaliter alliter*! And yet the Creator will not have it so, but yearns to be united with it, to be "at one" with it, to be "all and in all," etc.

In other words, with is the only preposition that will serve this theory of reality, because it contains both the idea of sameness and the idea of difference, both being together and being apart. To put it more succinctly still, with is the preposition that belongs to the language of love. Love means difference: I am not you, and you are not me; and if we *love* each other it does not mean (what it means in some ancient and also modern mysticism) that we simply merge into an ontic unity (John and Mary when they marry do not become Jarry!) Love means, rather, I am with you and you are with me in a special sense. We evoke each other's individual potentiality for being. We do not disappear into each other (love of the disappearing-into variety has usually meant that the weaker—naturally the female!—disappears into the stronger); rather, we become all the more present, real, solid as persons, individuals. What is broken—what disappears—is not our individual Thou-ness, but the hostility, the bid for self-sufficiency and permanence that kept us from loving each other.

Love, then, which *is* the fundamental ontology of the tradition of Jerusalem,[15] needs this preposition "with": not "above", and not "in" but "with." The German word invented by Heidegger—*Mitsein*—should be taken over by Christian theology (in any case the idea behind it came to Heidegger from that source!). *Being* (the fundamental philosophic category) is not just "being" in the tradition of Jerusalem; it is *being-with* (Mitsein). All that *is* exists under the mandate of its Creator, that it seek out and dwell with—and love!—everything else that *is*. Our being as human beings is a being-with; and the distortion of our being (Sin) is precisely our alienation from all that we are created to be "with". Sin is being-alone, being-against.

In its better expressions, Christian theology has known how to express all this with respect to two of the dimensions of our human relatedness: God, and our human partners ("the neighbor"). But Christian theology has rarely explored the meaning of these fundamental ontological assumptions for the third dimension of our threefold relatedness, our relation to the nonhuman world, the inarticulate creation. This is now what must be explored.

As the *Mitsein* of the ontology of love applies to our human relation to the nonhuman world, it contains the same two polar movements that are found in the other dimensions of our relatedness: One pole of this dialectic contains the thought of human *difference* from the other creatures. We cannot escape this, no matter how romantically attached we may be to the idea of humanity's being part of nature. According to the biblical witness we are different. Difference does not mean superiority. It does mean that we are more complex, more versatile, and certainly more vulnerable than the others. But why? Not so that we can lord it over them! Rather, so that we can exercise a unique responsibility towards them, a unique *answerability for* them. We are (yes, why should we not use this word?) to "have dominion." But what does that mean in the full perspective of biblical religion? Does it mean only what the word *literally* connotes? Trampling and being heavy-handed and dominating? Why should it? Why should we want to be so *literal*? Who (biblically speaking) is our *model* of dominion? Is it Caesar? The Pharoah? or even the divinely-approved Cyrus? No, it is the one whom we call "Lord"—*Dominus*: Jesus the Christ . . . "and him crucified"! *His* dominion, far from being a trampling over everybody and everything, seems to have involved his being trampled upon—as in the beautiful story of Shusaku Endo.[16]

So yes, we are different from the beasts of the field and the birds of the air. Let us not be romantic and imagine that we can just melt into nature! We have a reflective side that the other creatures do not have. It is harder for us to die than it is for them. We have always to choose, or to be the victims of our lack of choice. But the purpose of all this is that we should have [Jesus Christ's kind of] dominion: that is, that we should be servants, keepers, priests in relation to them. We are there to represent the others before their Maker and to represent to them—in our care of them—their Maker's care. We are the place where the creation becomes reflective about itself. The point at which it speaks—sings! *Homo loquens.* But we do not speak for ourselves—not when we are true to our essence, to the ontology of love. We speak for all of them, for the totality. And when we really do speak *for them*, not just to hear ourselves talk, what we say, what we shall perhaps one day say without reservation or qualification, is simply: "Thank you." Or, to put it less sermonically: *Gratitude* alone authenticates any human claim to "dominion." Until that gratitude has permeated our being wholly, unambiguously, "the whole creation groaneth."

But the other side of this dialectic has already been implied. We can only be the keepers and priests of the others if we are in some sense also *the same* as they are. We share their mortality, their limitations of power, their finitude. We can only represent them because we participate in the same creatureliness as they. If we are different, it is so that we may perceive and speak out of what is both their and our condition. "We perceive in order to participate, not in order to dominate."[17] Our representation of the inarticulate creation depends upon perception and reflection; but it also depends upon participation. One side demands the other.

And this brings us at last to the symbol that we have hardly named in this discussion of the relation between humanity and nature; we have not named it, but it has been the very presence around which the whole discussion has been woven, as the chapter heading suggests: stewardship. There is no other symbol in biblical literature, perhaps there is no other symbol in all of human literature, that so appropriately catches the two sides of this dialectical tension of which we have been speaking. The steward symbol is in the category of the metaphoric what the preposition "with" is in the realm of the linguistic. One does not have to go outside the symbol itself to do justice to the two dimensions and their complex interrelatedness.

On the one hand, the steward is singled out for a special responsibility. The steward is different. Unlike the other servants, the steward is truly answerable for what happens in the household. All the same, the steward is one of the others, by no means superior to them, having no absolute rights over them, liable to judgment because of his treatment of them. The steward is different, but the steward is also the same. Like all the others, the steward is recipient of that which can never be his/hers.

It is no wonder then that an increasing number of ecologists and others, many of whom have no personal relation to the Christian faith, find in this Judeao-Christian symbol one of the most profound metaphors of what is best in the Western world by way of stating a viable concept of the relation between humanity and nature. One of these persons writes:

> . . . .although much in Christianity has rightly been found by critics to be ecologically objectionable (in that nature is almost completely desacralized and man given quaisi-total dominion over creation), others

point out with equal correctness that *stewardship and other Christian virtues could easily form the basis of an ecological ethic.*[18]

This *could* happen. The condition for its actually doing so has a good deal to do with how we Christians handle our own tradition. In the foregoing chapters we have seen something of our neglect and misuse of this symbol. Our first responsibility as Christian stewards today may be to become better stewards of the stewardship idea itself!

5 From Symbol to Political Necessity

When we speak of stewardship as the key to the relation between humanity and nature we are speaking of a vision. Under the conditions of history, this vision is never fully realized. It is an eschatological vision, the vision of a state of final reconciliation, in which the enmity between creature and Creator, creature and creature, creature and creation will have given way to true mutuality and love: "being with."

It was this visionary aspect of our stewardship that the great American painter Edward Hicks (1780-1849) tried to express in his 'Peaceable Kingdom.' As James Thomas Flexner writes, Hicks . . .

... painted many Peaceable Kingdoms illustrating the biblical prophecy that the lion and the lamb shall lie down together. Not the lax sermons of conventional moralists, these pictures do not ignore the problem of evil. Hicks, who fought daily engagements with his own passions, knew that it would not be easy for the lion and the lamb to lie down together . . .[19]

and, we might add, it would be even more difficult for the child of Adam and Eve to lead them!

But while this is and remains an eschatological vision, it is not merely an *ideal*, an impossible dream. Today it has become the only real alternative. To continue trying to be nature's "lords and possessors" can only mean the end of the Experiment, for our lording and mastering has become increasingly bellicose. There is much revenge in it. On the other hand, to adopt the solution of the romantics and disappear *into* nature may solve the problem for the cockroaches, but what about the future Mozarts? The *only* way is to search our hearts, our pasts, and our present for clues as to how we might be in the world without simply being of it; how we might think, and make, and do, without through our thinking and making and doing destroying the very fragile craft that is our home. Stewardship is no longer just a nice ideal. It has become a social and political necessity.

VIII STEWARDSHIP AND THE QUEST FOR WORLD PEACE

1 The Primacy of This Issue

The three issues treated in this concluding part of our discussion on the meaning of Christian stewardship are of course not three separable issues but part of a whole—an unwelcome seamless robe that has been cast over the shoulders of our late 20th century civilization. The greatest difficulty in comprehending them, quite apart from trying to act responsibly in relation to them, is their intricate and confounded interwovenness. It is tempting to become fixated upon one of them. For instance many persons who are concerned primarily for the issue discussed in Chapter VI tend to overlook the fact that our planet will not sustain the kinds of demands that would be entailed if all earth's peoples were to emulate the rich, developed nations. Conversely, ecologists and others whose primary *entree* into the world *problematique* is the natural universe and humanity's desecration of nature tend to hold out for the preservation of nature at the expense of human survival, sometimes ending in a pessimism about the human race equalled only by the Augustinian-Calvinist tradition of "total depravity."

In a similar act of reductionism, those most preoccupied by the struggle for world peace sometimes manifest a naiveté respecting both human and natural issues, and in their zeal for the tactics of peace seem willing to sacrifice centuries of hard-won values.

What this complexity signifies, beyond that all simple solutions are to be distrusted implicitly, is the prodigious need today for a *forum* of analysis, reflection, and action, where the expertise of many disciplines can be in constant dialogue, and can inform the passion of many and often disparate groupings who are committed to this world. The university, as the name itself implies, came into being for something like that purpose. But our modern 'multiversities' have too much in common with the biblical Babel to function effectively as such forums. It should no longer be taken for granted even that *dialogue* of an interdisciplinary nature will occur in the universities, let alone that they will promote action designed to preserve and enhance the life of the world. Increasingly the forum springs into existence outside or alongside the established institutions, either in response to some specific need or spontaneously.

For Christians this ought to raise the question (which I have already broached in Chapter V) whether the Christian *koinonia* could not do more to foster such dialogue and mutual action. After all, what prevents it more than anything else (as anyone who lives and works in the university setting today knows perfectly well) is lack of trust and the fear of involvement. People who are competent to inform their neighbors about the physical properties of modern weaponry and warfare, environmental issues, resources, demography, etc., feel an inherent alienation within their communities of learning, government, or business. The message given off by the very atmosphere of our institutions is: "Do not tell us any sad stories. We are comfortable, well-paid, well-adjusted people. You can't expect us to solve the problems of the world!" Consequently, the passionate amongst the experts (often they are individuals who have become passionate about the world in spite of themselves!) are regularly driven outside the established institutions into the community of like-minded persons, with the result that *inter*disciplinary dialogue is again thwarted and the world again interpreted through the focus of one particular discipline, issue, or commitment. The Christian community—the church!—is called to be, and *can* be a place of reconciliation, where trust between persons is being learned, where those who are "many" may begin nonetheless to act as "one body." Making good this identity as the *soma Christou* today could mean, quite concretely, fostering and *being* zones of trust for precisely these world issues whose interrelatedness is so vexing. What more explicit application of the stewardship vocation of the Christian community could we wish for?[1]

The quest for world peace, then, is one of a whole spectrum of struggles, each of whose solution entails a continuing vigilance with respect to its effect upon all the others. Nothing is more to be feared today than the solutions of those who do not know what the problem is—that is, those who naively identify the problem with this or that aspect of the problem, as if the hydra could be killed by cutting off one of its heads!

Having said that, I must nevertheless insist that the quest for world peace requires our *primary* attention. It is by no means *separable* from the other dimensions of our total *problematique;* but it nevertheless has priority for our stewardship because of the sheer immediacy of the threat against which it is directed. As the Reverend Theodore Hesburgh of Notre Dame University recently stated that matter: "The world's other problems become meaningless if we don't solve this one—and do it quickly."[2] It should indeed be regarded as a sufficient test of the authenticity of our Christian claims to ask one another: Does your stewardship express itself in thought, word, and deed aimed at establishing the peace of this world? Without this, all the other acts of Christian stewardship are rendered presumptuous. For if peace cannot be assumed (and it cannot!), then neither justice for the Third World nor the creation of new attitudes towards the Natural World can have any lasting significance.

One of the principles we established in Chapter V was that of futurization. Our stewardship of Earth is not only for today, nor until the next election, nor even the next generation; it is for a future stretching out for a long, unknown period. For all practical purposes, it is forever! For the rest of time, humanity must live with the possibility of annihilation, and it taxes the imagination to wonder whether the human race will find the wisdom, endurance, and courage needed to stave off that possibility even for the next century. In an article provocatively entitled, "Nuclear Nemesis: Are There Enough Good People to Avoid Destruction?",[3] Gerald Barnes gave voice to the fear that lurks in the hearts of us all: "We have incontravertible and growing evidence," he wrote, "that Homo sapiens is too profit-motivated, too ignorant, too irresponsible, too fallible to handle plutonium without eventual—and repeated—catastrophe." As the statement implies, it is not only nuclear *warfare* that threatens this destruction but the whole thirst for this new toy, including also its supposedly peaceful uses.

The annihilation that is contemplated is no longer a divinely ordained apocalypse, which could fire the imagination of the ages because it somehow *confirmed* the race's presupposition of ultimate meaning and righteous judgment. The annihilation *we* live with, in contrast to our medieval and earlier forebears, is just a dreadful halt, a screaming termination, a million Hiroshimas.

> The atom bomb is today the greatest of all menaces to the future of mankind. In the past there have been imaginative notions of the world's end; its imminent expectation for their generation was the ethically and religiously effective error of John the Baptist, Jesus, and the first Christians. But now we face the real possibility of such an end. The possible reality which we must henceforth reckon with—and reckon with, at increasing pace of developments in the near future—is no longer a fictitious end of the world. It is no world's end at all, but the extinction of life on the surface of the planet.[4]

No doubt one reason why so many of us have 'stopped worrying and learned to love the Bomb' is the sheer incapacity of the average mind to grasp the dimensions of such an ending, or even the scientific data and the technology of its genesis. Even highly trained intelligences boggle at the thing; for not only does C.P. Snow's "Two Cultures" syndrome pertain here, but, since we are virtually being asked to contemplate nothingness, we are reminded of our inherent incapacity for such contemplation. We cannot even imagine the death of individuals, especially our own; how then could we place before our mind's eye the spectre of a lifeless planet?

The facts, especially if they are translated into imaginative lay language, go a little way towards comprehension, to be sure; and therefore Christian stewardship today must mean, in part, the stewarding of the *data* of war—something that the Christian church both can and must do more faithfully than agencies having no special commitment to life. These data need to be transmitted in ways that are once graspable and portable. Few ordinary mortals can understand the physical dynamics of nuclear fission, but most of us can comprehend statistics like the following:

- The standard bomb today is one megaton.
- One megaton means seventy times the power of the bomb dropped on Hiroshima.
- It is the equivalent of one million tons of TNT.
- If you put that much TNT into box cars, the train would be 200 miles long.
- Ten megatons is more than all the explosives used in World War II.
- Twenty megatons is more than all the explosives *ever* used!

Or this:

Every community with a population of over 50,000 is a probable traget for destruction in nuclear war. Those burned will have to contend with radiation, fallout, burned and dying refugees, etc. The high risk areas in the United States, by a conservative U.S. government estimate, include 400 targets.

Short-term radioactive fallout at the level of at least 100 rems would engulf most of the continental United States. Over the long term the effect would be virtually universal.

Try Toronto. A typical modern bomb would kill up to two million people. Other results: a crater one-half mile in diameter destroyed buildings up to a four-mile radius, a fire-storm igniting houses and trees for up to a 20-mile radius, blindness from the fireball for all those up to 40 miles, burns, radiation, sickness, death . . .[5]

Or again:

According to the most recent government figures, the United States now has enough nuclear warheads stashed in underground silos, on nuclear submarines and in sophisticated jets around the globe to launch an all-out attack which would kill every man, woman and child in the world twelve times over. The Pentagon says that if a total nuclear war did break out, between 95 million and 120 million Americans would die immediately in the exchange, with millions upon millions of others dying in the days and weeks following the holocaust. Despite the insanity of maintaining a nuclear arsenal of over 30,000 warheads, our government continues to build three new warheads every twenty-four hours. Worldwide expenditure on armaments now amounts to a staggering 400 billion dollars a year—most of it being spent by the two superpowers.[6]

But even such well-packaged, portable information fails to convey the reality of the nuclear madness. Art, poetry, and drama are perhaps better; but, as Jim Douglas poignantly states the problem in the following 'poem,' there is a built-in psychic block to our comprehension where this issue is concerned:

TRIDENT

What is Trident?
Trident is a nuclear submarine being built now
which will be able to destroy 408 cities or areas
at one time, each with a blast five times more powerful
than the Hiroshima bomb.
TRIDENT is 2,040 Hiroshimas.
One Trident submarine can destroy any country on earth.
A fleet of TRIDENT submarines (30 are planned)
can end life on earth.
How can anyone understand that?

Begin with a meditation:
To understand TRIDENT, say the word 'Hiroshima.'
Reflect on its meaning for one second.
Say and understand 'Hiroshima' again.
And again.
And again.
2,040 times.

Assuming you are able to understand 'Hiroshima' in
    one second, you will be
able to understand TRIDENT in 34 minutes.
That is one TRIDENT submarine
To understand the destructive power of a whole fleet
    of TRIDENT submarines
it would take you 17 hours, devoting one second to
    each 'Hiroshima.'
Your meditation is impossible.
To understand 'Hiroshima' alone
would take you a lifetime.

In short, the inherent *skandalon* to the intellect where the nuclear issue is concerned is its abstractness. We live in a time when "what is most *real* is most *abstract*."[7] The abstract has always presented grave, and perhaps finally insurmountable problems to the human intelligence. How much more is this the case in a society like our own, which for centuries now has given itself to empiricism in observation and functionalism in thought.

2 The Question at the Core of the Enigma

While we may be incapable of contemplating the Nihil, however, we are perhaps not incapable of contemplating the Question that is put to us by the prospect of worldly annihilation. At least Christians ought still to possess a certain aptitude for this Question, for it is the question that inheres (as we have said) in the core of our kerygma, the question to which the Cross of Jesus Christ speaks directly and decisively. In the Cross, God, for His part, declares Himself unambiguously and finally with respect to this question. The Cross means: *God loves this world.*

The followers of the Cross have never been quite so sure that they could say 'Amen' to that. We have vacillated, hesitated. Maybe, maybe not. We have taken refuge in sophisticated dialectics. Well, that is understandable enough: it is a terribly costly thing to love this world. It is not simple, either; because love must never mean *mere* acceptance!

But now the Question is put to us again. The threat of the *kind* of ending implicit in the nuclear madness poses to Christian faith perhaps its greatest historical challenge. For in the face of that prospect we are under obligation as never before to declare clearly and without reservation whether this world matters to us, and matters ultimately. The whole course of 2,000 years gathers itself in this single issue and puts to the hesitating, ambiguous, and covertly *docetic* faith that we represent the Question: Do you or do you not care about *this world*? 'The Bomb' is thus not only a real (i.e. physical) threat to our world; it is also a symbolic threat to all who have been less than capable of loving this world. Since the means are now at hand *implement* human hate, revenge, and lovelessness in relation to this world, nothing can prevent this implementation from being deployed except a change of heart on the part of the world's human inhabitants. What we are asked (if I may again try to phrase this outrageous Question!) is *not merely whether we are against the destruction of the world but whether we love it*! Only a few bold egos have ever been found who would actually name themselves "nihilists," or even "anarchists"! The problem is not the nihilists but (to use Nietzsche's other category) "the last men"—the people who for the sake of the private "happiness" they have "invented" do not bother themselves with ultimate questions. Alas there are many of them in the churches—and what is worse they are using the faith of the Cross to shore up their "happiness"! *They* certainly don't want the world destroyed! No, but neither will they dare to expose themselves long enough to its pain to give a thought to its healing. They do not love it. Perhaps they do not love anything, though the *idea* of love charms them. Christian stewardship is not about lovely ideas. Its basis in reality is not a sentiment but an Event: "Jesus Christ and him crucified." It is into this Event that we are baptized—into *this* stewardship that we are being incorporated. 'The Bomb' is a symbolic form of the question that God has always put to his people: Will you be baptized with my baptism? Will you take up your cross? Will you also love? Simon Peter, do you *love* me?

We Christians come to this decisive moment with a very shaky past. For not only fringe Christianity but in one way or another almost all the historic forms of our faith have manifested a strange

119

fascination for 'the End' of the world. This fascination stems partly from the belief, which seems to have informed the earliest congregations, that the coming Kingdom necessitates the destruction of Earth and the cessation of time. It is also in part of course that distaste for matter, coming to us from our Hellenistic past and expressing itself (as we noted in the Bonhoeffer reference[8]) in the displacement of a theology of resurrection by a non-Hebraic theology of "immortality" of the soul. Only Christian Liberalism of the 19th and early 20th centuries tried to translate into historical, earthly terms the biblical symbol of the heavenly Kingdom. But as we have seen, Liberalism tied its expectations so uncritically to the aspirations of Modern Western society that when that society faltered and the religion of Progress gave way to the quest for sheer survival, the Liberal version of the heavenly Kingdom was widely rejected as naive and utopian. Ever since the First World War, Christian theology has tended (in reaction to a failed Liberal optimism) to remove the Kingdom of God farther and farther away from anything that could ever find realization under the conditions of time and space. The numerical victory in North America today of those forms of Christianity most characterized by otherworldly apocalypticism is only a stage—perhaps not the last one—in this evolution of non-worldly "spiritualism." Apocalyptic sectarianism is the visible tip of an ecclesiastical iceberg. Why, otherwise, did we all feel judged by the Jonestown horror? The dying curse of the demented Jim Jones came too close for comfort: "I would like to see the whole thing come to a screaming end!"

3 "Thy Kingdom Come, Thy Will be *Done On Earth* . . . "

There is no doubt truth in the insistence of post-Liberal Christianity that the divine Kingdom must remain a vision and a symbol, and not become a blueprint for political realities. The history of Christendom is strewn with the wrecks of "heavenly Kingdoms"—including the one that began in New England! Certainly some of the most intolerable states in history have been produced by persons who imagined their ideology to be, not the product of human dreaming and scheming, but the very model of heavenly Jerusalem! However much we may admire from afar the "theocratic" state Calvin and his colleagues tried to set up in 16th Century Geneva, no one who lives in contemporary North America, not even the most ardent Calvinist, would have found that city blessed!

Yet there is an opposite danger, and it is perhaps the primary one for most of those who will read these pages. I mean the danger of regarding the symbol of the Kingdom in such 'poetic' terms that in the end one falls into that same docetism that we have chastised here, that spiritualization of the faith that is the undoing of genuine

Christian stewardship. If we are to struggle against our own Christian otherworldly past, as well as against the narcissistic inner-worldliness of our present secular society, then we must learn again for our time how to let this 'unattainable' vision of God's righteous Reign shape our thinking and our acting within the world. So long as we are prepared to continue praying *that* prayer—"Thy Kingdom come, they will be done on earth . . ."—we are making ourselves responsible as Earth stewards for the blessedness of this world. The rejection of Liberalism, which is still rather unaccountably fashionable in some circles, ought at last to give way to a respect for what the Liberals in general and the Social Gospelers in particular were trying to do: make the gospel what it is, viz. a *worldly* statement. The sin for which we shall be held responsible is not sin against God (an abstract and religious thing) but sin against God's beloved world:

> God can be hated and given offense only in man. Sin is not to be understood in a special religious sense as the lack of love *for God* or as rebellion against a master, but it must be thought of in worldly and political categories. Neither the desecrated temple nor the declining churches are our accusers, but the situation of the world.[9]

Translating the stewardship of the Kingdom into the terms of our own context means, certainly, that we must be much more skeptical of worldly ideologies than our Liberal forebears were—of the ideologies of *all* the worlds, First, Second, and Third. We shall exercise a healthy cynicism about solutions, lasting peace, war to end war (especially when it means "limited nuclear war to end war!"), etc. But we shall also set our faces against those who write off the earth and look for heavenly solace to earthly grief.

Unlike our Liberal foreparents, our stewardship will steer clear of the dreamers of 'perfect peace'—"where there is no peace." Nevertheless we shall imitate the best of those hopeful Christians by our refusal to settle for whatever forms the "no peace" wants to assume—in our refusal to accept the status quo of arms races, cold wars, bogged-down negotiations, brinkmanship, refusal to dialogue, etc., etc. We reject this status quo! For we are stewards, and by now it is perfectly clear to us (what was not after all *quite* clear to our forebears) that the acceptance of the status quo means the acceptance of death, the meaningless and agonizing death of worlds:

Status Quo

Wer will das die Welt
soll bleib wie sie ist,
der will das die Welt
nicht bleibt.[10]

4 The Divine Imperative: An End to Docetism!

"Nothing in our time is more dubious, it seems to me," wrote Hannah Arendt in her essay on Lessing, than our attitude towards the world, nothing less to be taken for granted than that concord with what appears in public which an honor imposes on us, and the existence of which it affirms . . .

> In our century even genius has been able to develop only in conflict with the world and the public realm, although it naturally finds, as it always has done, its own peculiar concord with its audience. But the world and the people who inhabit it are not the same. The world lies between people, and this in-between . . . is today the object of the greatest concern and the most obvious upheaval in almost all the countries of the globe. Even where the world is still halfway in order, or is kept halfway in order, the public realm has lost the power of illumination which was originally part of its very nature. More and more people in the countries of the Western world, which since the decline of the ancient world has regarded freedom from politics as one of the basic freedoms, make use of this freedom and have retreated from the world and their obligations within it. This withdrawal from the world need not harm an individual; he may even cultivate great talents to the point of genius and so by a detour be useful to the world again. But with each such retreat an almost demonstrable loss to the world takes place; what is lost is the specific and usually irreplaceable in-between which should have formed between this individual and his fellow men.[11]

The specific thoughts and deeds that make for the world's peace cannot be set forth in a program. The stewarding of a world on the brink of disaster, like the care of a patient in the crisis of a dread illness, must be moment-to-moment. Moreover, to carry the metaphor a little farther, as the tending of the ill patient requires the expertise and labor of a whole hospital staff, so the tending of a sick world must be a team effort. Christians can perhaps, as Christians, contribute little more than passionate dedication to the intricate task of keeping such a world alive.

But that is the point! We cannot as Christians dictate policies and engineer negotiations and make decisions concerning the technicalities of arms reduction and so on—though many of those who in their vocations and professions do such things are avowed Christians, and can presumably draw certain conclusions from that! But *as Christians* we can do something—*be* something—far more significant in the longrun; something which, unless it is done, will prevent all the other, practical things from being done. This namely: We can determine that we shall not any longer be amongst those who are ambiguous about the world, who withdraw from it, and whose withdrawal results in "an almost demonstrable loss to the world." This is the *sine qua non* of all activity directed towards world peace today. Even if we devote much time and energy to the peace movement; even if we march with the marchers and contribute our money; even if we give our bodies to be burned "but have not love," love for the world, it will be as "nothing."

An end to Christian docetism is the divine imperative that is contained in the dread nuclear data of our epoch. If that imperative were obeyed, even by a minority of the followers of Jesus Christ, there could be a demonstrable gain to the whole movement for peace. If as stewards we make this first and most rudimentary step towards tending God's garden wilderness—that is, declare our love for it—we shall have leapt over a chasm that has long separated us from those who lie in Abraham's bosom.

IX ON BEING STEWARDS

1 A Manner of Speaking

We have seen that stewardship does not describe any one dimension of the Christian life, it describes the whole posture called 'Christian.' Through this metaphor, the biblical authors with their genius for images found a single term that could point simultaneously to all three foci of Christian faith—its orientation to Him whose mastery the steward acknowledges; its orientation to other human beings who participate in the universal stewardship of "the speaking animal"; its orientation towards the nonhuman creatures and towards Earth, their common home.

There is of course no need to make extraordinary claims for the metaphor as such. It is not the only way in which the first witnesses to the grace in which we stand articulated their conception of our faith. It is not even the most important amongst them. In comparison with many other images and ideas that have made their impact upon historic Christianity (*soma Christou*, "bride of Christ," "ambassadors for Christ," "witnesses," "kingdom of priests," etc.) the metaphor of the steward is perhaps even of minor importance.

But images have their time and place. Symbols, we have noticed, are not created, they occur. They are born and they die; unlike signs, they cannot be arbitrarily chosen or dispensed with. For certain ages of the church, the terms referred to above, along with many others that could be named, were lively and immediate symbols: they were sufficiently related to the fundamental structures, beliefs, hopes, fears, and values of the societies in which they were current to make their use both meaningful to believers and comprehensible to unbelief. Some of the terms to which I am referring still have currency today, and some of them belong so essentially to the Story that Christians tell that they can never be given up. Yet it is also true that a great many of the categories that historic Christianity has used to describe the *being* of Christians are less than accessible to our present-day understanding. They may sometimes be *made* meaningful, if they are sufficiently interpreted, illustrated, and illuminated by reference to other categories that 20th century people *can* grasp. But they do not speak to us directly, as they did to some of our forebears.

Take a category like 'priesthood.' The fact that the term 'priest' is still used daily to describe an important office in the Church of Rome, the Anglican/Episcopal communion, and Orthodox churches may or may not help to make it accessible as a way of depicting the being and calling of all Christians, corporately and individually. I suspect that on the whole it inhibits the latter use of the term, since it seems so obviously to designate a particular and unique person and function. But Protestants are hardly more blest when it comes to the modern communicative potential of this ancient and important biblical term. Some Protestants will tell you that the whole Reformation of the 16th century was fought over the issue of "the priesthood of all believers" (which is not true); but when they proceed to define what precisely that means they are usually less than articulate, to say the least. The notion that we are priests *to one another*, responsible for each other's well-being, representative of each other before God and of God to each other—this is hardly the average Protestant's work-a-day self-image! True enough, it must in some way *become* our self-understanding if we are to make good something approaching Christian maturity. But few of our contemporaries, I suspect, will arrive at that maturity through the contemplation of the traditional category of 'priesthood,' indispensable as this category is.

Stewardship, as I have been at some pains to show, is certainly not without its problems, either—particularly within the church itself, where it is too narrowly associated with finances. Yet there is a sufficient openness to the larger meaning of the term in our society as a whole that it is, it seems to me, redeemable within the churches as well. Secular or nonreligious interest in the symbol serves to remind Christians of the deeper significance of a concept they have carried through the years. "If the children are silent, the very stones cry out!" In the foregoing, I have tried to show that what this symbol stands for by way of a human posture or *imago hominis* is not only *pertinent* to our situation but must be regarded as a 'necessity laid upon us.' But even at the linguistic level, the term has achieved in our time a certain apologetic coinage. It is found as often on the lips of persons outside the churches as within them. (Just as I was composing these thoughts, I came across the term "stewardship" twice in an issue of *Newsweek*—in the political section!). The fact that the term also signifies commonplace work such as that of airline stewardesses and stewards should not worry us. Some of the most honored metaphors of the faith (shepherd, teacher, disciple, bridegroom, judge, friend, etc.) have their origins in just such everyday offices. It will certainly not hinder the communicability of the idea that airplane personnel are good-natured people who look after other people. In some tangible linguistic sense, then, as well as in terms of its deeper meaning, the metaphor of the steward has blossomed. It describes a way of being Christian that is somehow apologetically "ripe."

2 "The Stewardship of All Believers"

Not only is stewardship a word that our world uses and in some measure grasps, it also has apologetic possibilities because of the fact that it does—or can do—justice to important dimensions of the Christian message, including Christian *self*-understanding. There are two reasons for this: (1) It conveys what is essential in much of the tradition, including ideas that were conveyed in conventional terms whose coinage is questionable today; (2) It does this *without* carrying with it in the process some of the injurious or misleading connotations of "older" categories.

To consider the latter aspect first: Some of the conventional language used to depict the life and work of Christians, when it is not simply mystifying (even to Christians), implies often certain qualities that constitute barriers both to communication and community. Frequently of course these undesirable qualities have been put upon the terms in question by centuries of ecclesiastical malpractice. By association, they have become humorous, presumptuous, pretentious, offensive, etc. Theologians and "preachers" (sic!) still use them (one has to, of course), but even in the act of stating them one often cringes inwardly—especially if one is using them outside the "household of God" (sic!). A phrase like "Christian witnesses" for example has a slight but unmistakable tinge of self-righteousness about it. To exchange it for "proclaimers of the Word" is to jump from the frying pan into the fire. "Ambassadors for Christ" was excellent in the Pauline context, perhaps; but ambassadors nowadays have a high reputation for official stuffiness, when they are not perceived as mere functionaries of State. "People of the Way," "the Community of the Cross," "the pilgrim people,"—such concepts are in my opinion better (because less triumphalistic) ways of describing the being of Christians; but they are all of them in-church phrases, as are so many of the New Testament metaphors, including the most famous one, "Body of Christ."

The most objectionable aspect of a number of the terms by which we conventionally designate ourselves as Christians is of course that (to the nonchurched at least) they smack of a false security, superiority, and authority. Just try using what was one of the most common categories employed by our Puritan and other ancestors in North America ("The Elect of God") at the next community meeting or Brotherhood Week! We all know Christians who persist in naming themselves "The Saved," to the continuing consternation of "The Damned"; but the offensive nature of Christian self-description is not limited to biblicist and fundamentalist religion. Even our more "bourgeois Christian" appellations—not only the category "priesthood" but also the less definitive "ministry"—carry with them a sufficient degree of holier-than-thouness that they readily function as 'false scandals' (Bultmann) to communication and community. In particular, they suggest a certain *authority*—more precisely pretention to authority—that immediately puts the world on the defensive (including that world from which priests and ministers so often distinguish themselves, the Christian Laity!)

It is precisely the nonsacrosanct, nonauthoritarian character of the steward that commends it, on the 'negative' side. Of course any *word*, through bad practice, can become tainted. But while the steward metaphor has been truncated, it has not I think been tainted. I mean that it has not been made to serve the characteristically triumphalistic assumptions about ourselves that have informed our whole history, especially from Constantine onwards. Like the general nomenclature of servanthood, of which it is after all a specific application and nuance, the symbol of the steward militates *against* its co-optation by Power. There is an implicit modesty in it, and this makes it much more compatible with the "theology of the Cross" than many and perhaps most of the concepts by which Christians have identified themselves. Even priesthood, which is of course much better in this respect than the kingship nomenclature (from which *very* imperialistic self-images have been derived by Christians)—even priesthood, I say, can without great difficulty be co-opted by the triumphalist urge. The prophets of Israel knew that long ago! Glory has no doubt its place in the Christian story; but given our particular history it is hard for the world to separate Christian glory from Christian power. It behooves us therefore to explore what we mean by glory through the use of images (and of course deeds!) that clearly locate *power* elsewhere.

It is for this reason that stewardship can be perceived even by secular observers as an *alternative* to the power-pursuits of imperial Christianity. Insofar as the churches pursue the stewardship motif, Jeremy Rifkin believes, they convey an entirely new and different image, both of being Christian and of being human:

> Stewardship requires that human kind respect and conserve the 'natural' workings of God's order. The natural order works on the principles of diversity, interdependence and decentralization. Maintenance replaces the notion of progress, stewardship replaces ownership and nurturing replaces engineering. Biological limits to both production and consumption are acknowledged; the principle of balanced distribution is accepted; and the concept of wholeness becomes the essential guideline for measuring all relationships and phenomena.

> In reality, then, the new stewardship doctrine represents a fundamental shift in humanity's frame of reference. It establishes a new set of governing principles for how human beings should behave and act in the world. As a world view, the stewardship doctrine demands of the faithful an uncompromising adherence. . . .

> ... The new concept is that dominion is stewardship rather than ownership and conservation rather than exploitation. ... This new emphasis on stewardship is providing the foundation for the emergence of a second Protestant reformation and a new covenant vision for society.[1]

The apologetic coinage of the stewardship symbol is due however to positive as well as negative considerations. Not only does it guard against injurious and misleading images of the Christian/human life; it also conveys the essential meaning of some—not all—of the important traditional categories by which Christians have identified themselves and their mission. Here I am thinking especially of that biblically and traditionally so important term, priesthood. I am certainly not advocating that this category be dropped from the church's vocabulary. It will continue to be meaningful within all the great divisions of the ecumenical church. It is indeed *for the sake of that meaning* that I would propose—not the substitution, but—the addition or supplementation of stewardship.

In the most provocative and even exciting ways, the steward metaphor can revive and preserve what is most precious and indispensable in the concept of priesthood. For like the latter concept, the symbol of the steward is at bottom a symbol of *representation*. Like the priest, the steward is a vicar, deputy, *Stellvertreter*. The authority he/she bears is wholly bound up with the One whose creation he/she tends; and, like the shepherd, the steward's "authority" is valid only when it is an adequate representation of the Creator's *love* for what He will have tended, 'kept.' The steward not only represents the loving Creator (Shepherd) to the creation; the steward also answers to the Creator in behalf of the other creatures, as the articulate center of the created order, the "speaking animal." There may indeed be *nuances* in the priest image that are not contained in that of the steward; but the essence of the office is the same. Both are mediatorial figures, both re-present God to the World and the World to God. Neither needs to be considered a replacement for the other. But the advantage of the steward symbol is that it has apologetic potential for communicating the essential and concrete meaning of Christian (and human) representation without conveying at the same time the narrowly sacerdotal connotations that, unfortunately, adhere to the office of priesthood.

What then if we spoke about "the *stewardship* of all believers"? I am almost positive that for many Protestants at least this could redeem a concept that, when stated literally in the Reformation language of priesthood, is remote and perhaps meaningless. (In truth, in its usually understood form it is downright deceptive, for its message to most Protestants is just the anti-Catholic idea, "I don't need a priest. I have direct access to the Almighty!") The very worldliness and concreteness of "the stewardship of all believers" puts flesh on the skeleton of a traditional idea. It brings the being and mission of Christians down to earth: their business is not just with God, and certainly it is not just the very private traffic with God connoted by the common misappropriation of the Reformation teaching. Their business is the being of stewards in all phases of their life, in their relationships with one another, in their everyday worldly existence. Through the symbol of the steward we might once again, especially as Protestants, find our way back to the real meaning of our corporate and personal priesthood.

3 A Way of *Being* Christian

It is essential to the realization of the potentiality present in this symbol however that it connotes a manner of *being*—and perhaps just here the biblical concept of *priesthood* could help, in turn, to prevent stewardship from signifying only a function, a work. Without conjuring up the whole tangled history of the meaning of priesthood, complete with the concept of indelible orders and the like, we may certainly affirm that priesthood as it is biblically conceived refers to something one *is* and not just something one does. The main point that Protestants would insist upon here is that the "one" in question is not just the ordained ministry but the whole people of God. But if that is understood, then we must certainly go on to say that "the whole people of God" as "a priestly people" is not called merely to do this or that, but to *be* a representative people in the world.

So stewardship must be understood first as descriptive of the being, the *life*, of God's people. *Deeds* of stewardship arise out of the *being* of the steward. It is no different here than it is elsewhere: the act is an expression and consequence of the life that enacts it. A parent does certain things with respect to his or her child because of the relationship in which the two stand. A musician must play or sing because the music is there, and will find its outlet. Jeremiah must prophesy because he has been grasped by divine Truth; when he tries to squelch the prophetic utterance it is as if his soul were on fire (Jeremiah 20). We are able to love, to perform deeds of love, because we are loved (I John 4). No doubt human beings do many things that do not emerge out of the depths of their being. We even try to perform 'loving' deeds when there is no real love in us. The world is full of nonmusical children and adults who, to please their parents or to win public approval, torture their souls and bodies in order to perform tolerably on instruments. And let us also admit that there are many would-be Jeremiahs who are not inspired (or afflicted!) with the Truth! All the same, the only authentic deeds, whether of love or art or truth, arise from souls and minds that have been inspired, who must give what they have received.

Stewardship honors this same law: the deed springs from the

gift—the gift of "new life." Unfortunately we have not understood this very well in the churches, and therefore many of us are stewards in the same manner as the parent who loves the child out of a sense of duty, or the musician who drums up a few boring pieces on the piano though he has no music in his soul. We regard stewardship as something you do rather than someone you are. I do not discount the possibility that, through doing, some may learn the deeper lesson of being the steward, just as some people become fairly good musicians through sheer determination and practice. But while that may *happen*, it should not be translated into ecclesiastical method. Real and effective deeds of stewardship will occur only when persons hear that gospel and are moved by that Spirit that changes their *being*, lifting them from the sloth of irresponsibility or judging their pride of mastery and giving them new being, the being of the steward.

And so we come to the bottom line: funding and filling the offices and handling the physical affairs of the church. I said that I do not intend to offer a program for Christian bookkeeping, but I do intend what I say here to be thought *entirely practical*. If what I have said in this immediate context about the being of the steward is true; and if the whole direction of this study has any significance at all, then the place to begin our lessons in stewardship is not with some of the *consequences* of the life of the steward, but with its genesis! Instead of periodic or regular efforts at conjuring up deeds of stewardship; instead of financial campaigns and bazaars and garage sales aimed at making temporary stewards out of essentially slothful or egotistical people; instead of cajoling and harping and bugging people to become Sunday School teachers or parish visitors or members of the official board, etc., etc.—in short, instead of working for the performance of the deed—we need to learn how to teach and preach the gospel and interpret the Christian *life as such* in terms of stewardship. The world is crying out for keepers and tenders of its wonderful, frail beauty; and God desires to send us out as stewards into this astonishing, unique creation of His. Until we have been grasped by that Word and Deed of our God; until we have begun to *be* who we are, then no amount of exhortation or "works" will alter greatly the image of the church or the course of the world.

4 Mission as a Function of Stewardship

The being of stewards is not only the vocation of individual Christians, it is the mission of the whole church. I want to accentuate the verb: stewardship *is* the church's mission. Rightly to understand the depths of this old/new symbol of the Christian life is to know that the mission of the church *is* its stewardship.

This may seem a shocking and even heretical claim in the light of that conventional logic (we spoke about it earlier) that insists that stewardship is the *means* (usually it is phrased "only the means") to the *end* of Mission. But in view of the holistic understanding of stewardship I have attempted to develop in this study I hope that such a claim could be received by many of my readers as the most obvious and necessary conclusion to all that has been said heretofore.

It is, I think, precisely because stewardship has been placed in such a subservient relation to mission that we have ended up with a truncated view of stewardship—and at a time in history when the world is ready to receive from us something far more radical! But now, in concluding this study, I want to suggest that our questionable prioritizing with respect to mission and stewardship has also resulted in a truncated and questionable understanding of the church's *mission*. Through a deeper comprehension of stewardship we can, I believe, arrive at an understanding of Christian Mission in the world that is both more appropriate to the *authentic* roots of our faith and more prophetic in relation to the Age in which we find ourselves.

(a) Mission and Stewardship in the Imperial Church: In order to demonstrate this thesis, I must ask the reader to recollect some aspects of our historical reflections in Chapter II. There we noted, as a matter entirely pertinent to our topic of stewardship, that in the year 313 the Emperor Constantine issued an edict of toleration in favor of the Christians, and that by the end of the same century *only* Christianity was legally permitted in the Western empire. From this point onwards, the *characteristic* forms of Christianity in the world have been "established" forms. That is to say, throughout approximately four-fifths of its history Christianity has existed chiefly as the official or semi-official religion of empires. One empire after another has courted this faith and been courted by it. When therefore we speak about Christianity—historically, phenomenologically, sociologically—we are speaking of an imperial religion.

Now in the constantinian situation, that is, wherever and however Christianity operates as the established cult of the dominant culture, *Mission* is *inextricably* bound up with power. It is necessary to discuss this from two complementary angles. On the one hand, the link between mission and power in the imperial church refers to the church's particular orientation towards the institutional and economic sources of power within the empire to which it is espoused. It must pay court to these sources for its continued existence and welfare as such a cult depends upon its acceptability to them. It sustains its own power by seeking and maintaining proximity to their power. Thus its "mission," which is to say its total witness, consists in large measure in its appeal to the dominant classes and the structures of authority operative in a given society. It may indeed play a significant role in society, as guardian of a higher morality, bearer of foundational traditions, and the place to which the human need for mystery and ritual may refer itself. Yet even at its best cultic Christianity walks a delicate tightrope between challenging the society and confirming it. Its challenge must never be felt as a contradiction of the overt values and practices of the ruling social strata. Thus it may plead for a *higher* morality, but not for an order of justice altogether different from the regnant systems of behavior.

This has to be seen as part of what is meant by the *mission* of the church in the imperial situation, because it not only requires the major portion of the energies of the church to sustain such a modus operandi with power, but it is altogether determinative for the rest of what mission means. It is hardly likely that a church that aligns itself with the primary powers of a society will preach to the rivals or potential enemies of those powers (including the lower classes within the same society) a gospel that might end by contradicting the aspirations of the ruling powers. To be sure, the gospel has sometimes foiled its own preachers and brought to the oppressed the very courage they needed to rise against their oppressors. As the Black community in the United States learned; as some of the indigenous peoples of North America have learned; as women in the churches have been finding out, it is hard to keep the revolutionary dimension out of the Christian story, even when it is passed along in platitudinous forms and as an opiate for anxious and bored souls. But imperial Christianity never *intends* this kind of spin-off. When it has happened, it has happened as a matter of "sheer grace"—and human embarrassment!

The second and more direct way in which mission is linked with the quest for power in the imperial church is that it is inevitably associated with the survival and expansion of the church as such. Without dramatizing the matter in the least, we could at this juncture reflect upon the centuries-long involvement of all forms of Christianity in the acquisition (often enough through devious and questionable means) of properties, treasures, resources, and "souls," all in the name of the Christian Mission. But we should not permit our critical analysis of imperial Christianity to become too much bound up with its lower manifestations. It is too simple to depict imperial Christianity's quest for power as if it were a sinister thing. Even where sinister or devious methods have been employed, the *motivation* has often been high, sometimes noble, given certain theological assumptions. Let us even admit that the imperial church is impelled by the desire, not primarily to secure *its own* power but rather to establish the power of *the gospel and the rule of Christ* in the lives of persons and societies.

But that does not make the power foundation of mission in the imperial church less questionable. Rather, it brings us to the heart of the more serious question. For what must be asked (what we must ask *ourselves* as Christians at this point in our pilgrimage) is whether it is in the first place our Lord's *will* that we gain this kind of power and ascendency for Him. The power foundation of mission in imperial Christianity is not to be questioned primarily because of the sinful *use* of power by the church, i.e. using it for its own direct aggrandizement. Rather, the question must be raised at the level of what has been our highest motivation. Imperial Christianity at its best has been impelled by the desire to "win the world for Christ." But does Christ want to win the world? Is it not possible that that kind of "winning" is in fundamental conflict with the purposes of our Lord? May it not be that what he himself said of individuals could apply equally to his church as a whole—namely that it would be possible to gain the whole world and lose the very soul, the very essence of the thing? Mission understood as winning, that is as mastery, simply does not fit the picture of the One who said plainly that he had come to serve, not to be served. Even therefore when it is the mastery *of the Christ* that is intended and not (not directly at any rate) ecclesiastical mastery, it is still mastery and not servanthood that informs this whole, deeply influtential tradition of Christian mission.

Given such a *missionary* presupposition, it was and is inevitable that *stewardship* could be present in imperial Christianity only in reductionist forms, as we have seen. It could never achieve the status of a basic orientation or even a major dimension in the life and work of the Christian churches. It could exist only at the ethical level and, at that, only as a kind of optional or fringe ethic for the enthusiastic. It could be the means, never the end.

This reductionist conception of stewardship is not accidental. Its presence amongst us still is not due to the fact that stewardship committees have failed to be enthusiastic enough in their educational and promotional campaigns. It is present as a direct consequence of our primary image of the church, including our missiology. So long as our understanding of the church and its task in the world is certainly informed by magisterial assumptions, stewardship can enter the life of the churches only in minimal and even trivialized forms.

For *the fundamental assumptions of stewardship* seriously *conceived are inimical to the monarchical conception of the church and its mission.* While mission under the conditions of constantinian Christianity must mean the expansion of Christian *mastery*, stewardship seriously conceived refers to a posture of radical *service*. While mission in the imperial church implies that the missionizing community is in possession of something not enjoyed by the others (truth, salvation, righteousness, etc.), stewardship in its very essence contains a polemic against the whole idea of possession, whether material or spiritual possession. While mission in Christendom has meant molding the wills and minds of persons and nations to preconceived states of spiritual and moral rectitude, stewardship implies the husbanding of the good wherever it is found, the midwifery of truth in all its varied manifestations. With stewardship conceived in Christian depth, the one who is to be served takes precedence over the one who serves. Not the gaining of influence, power, property, therefore; not the winning of souls and tongues to the Christian confession; not even (as an end in itself) the extension of the manifest Kingship of Christ in the world, but rather the care and nurture of life, the healing of the one who fell amongst thieves, the feeding of the hungry and freeing of the oppressed, the befriending of the friendless, the equitable distribution of earth's bounty, the passion for justice and peace, the dialogue with all who hunger and thirst for authenticity: *that* is the essential attitude of Christian stewardship. That is its peculiar *doxa*. It does not seek its glory in power; it does not even seek to establish the sovereignty of the God who commissions and sustains it (God does not need us to establish His sovereignty!). Rather it seeks to establish that which that God himself sought and seeks, in great humility, to establish: namely, the peace, abundance, and glory of the creation. Like God himself (Emmanuel!) the Christian steward is anthropocentric and geocentric!

In other words, stewardship means our incorporation into the being and working of the One who came to serve and not to be served, the Chief Steward Jesus. In the Protestant tradition it should not have to be said that this incorporation is a matter of *sola gratia, sola fide*—"not by works, lest any one should boast." We are orientated towards humanity and the biosphere, not because we are altruistic but because the grace by which we are being grasped *pushes us* towards the world and enables us to begin to act like loving servants instead of dominating masters. But let us not mistake it: this grace does not permit us to regard such stewardship as an option, or merely as one consequence of belief. It is at the center. It is a total attitude and orientation, not just an ethical addendum. It is a matter of *being*.

And precisely as such a total orientation stewardship contains an implicit and radical polemic against imperial Christianity and the interpretation and practice of mission that has informed imperial Christianity. Therefore stewardship as a serious, fundamental approach to the life of the Christian *koinonia* in the world throughout the greater share of its history, has never been able to achieve a lasting foothold in the church. The imperial church did not and does not have great difficulty perceiving its own triumphant image and goals in some of the New Testament's more aggressive and triumphalistic terms, especially its exhortation to world mission. Just think of the fate of a text like the so-called "Great Commission" at the end of Matthew's Gospel. As soon as the sociological conditions of the church were altered from the status of an illicit religion to that of the official cult of empire, Matthew's exhortation to "make disciples of all nations, baptizing them in the name of the Father and of the Son and of the Holy Spirit" could seem a veritable licence for the whole Christendom enterprise, even its most militant aspects. But the biblical concept of *stewardship* could never be adapted to constantinian religion. It could only be reduced and marginalized. For with the keen sense that power always has for sniffing out its own betrayal from within, imperial Christianity could easily recognize in the way of the steward, taken as a symbol for the whole behavior of the church in the world, as an altogether different route from the one it very early adopted.

(b) Stewardship and Mission in the Post-Constantinian Church: But it is just here that we may begin to reflect upon the second, *constructive* aspect of this analysis of the relation between mission and stewardship. For as we have remarked in the Introduction and at various points along the way, it is precisely that different route that opens up to the church today as its only authentic way into the future. Just at the point where imperial Christianity, embodying the way of mastery, has failed, this other route becomes available, viable, full of meaning. Of course it has always been there, and of course there have always been Christian minorities who knew of it and tried to follow it. But now it becomes for us *the only way*. For the other way, the old, broad way of triumphalistic Christendom, is already closed to us; more important and on the positive side, the world itself, having meantime been humbled by time, is vastly in need of the friendship of the steward.

Already at the outset of this study we introduced the theme of the death of Christendom. Christianity, having existed throughout most of its history as the religion of empire, finds itself being reduced to the status of one religious alternative amongst many others, and at a time when large numbers of earth's inhabitants doubt that any specifically *religious* alternative is either justifiable or necessary. Christianity is less influential at the end of the century that was supposed to have been "The Christian Century" than it was at the beginning. In many parts of the formerly Christian world, the church has been notoriously decimated. Even in avowedly Christian societies like ours, the tenets of Christianity are no longer regarded as obvious or axiomatic. Christian moral assumptions are having to vie with other alleged values on equal grounds, or perhaps with three strikes against them before they start. The most basic dogmas, stories, and myths of Christianity are now as obscure to the young as the teachings of Confucius or Greek mythology. In short, we are living in "the last days of the Constantinian Era" (Gunther Jacob).

This is not a new phenomenon. It is a process dating back to the breakdown of the Middle Ages and the dawning of the Age of Reason. But it has become a *conspicuous* phenomenon in the present century.

It is natural that this situation has produced a conservative reaction in the churches. As with all dying, one of the inevitable responses to the death of Christendom is denial. Not only are there many Christians who close their eyes to this sociological and historical phenomenon, being unable psychically to entertain the thought of an "unsuccessful" church; but there are many who, in the face of this ending, commit themselves with renewed vigor to the recovery of Christendom. Much contemporary "evangelism," with its bid for a Christian world by the year 2000 and so on, is inspired by that sort of last-ditch effort. And in "the Age of Uncertainty" (Galbraith) any ideology that can offer certitudes of the kind offered by biblical literalism and the like today will have no difficulty finding adherents. But no matter what temporary gains this kind of evangelism is able to make, the "end of the constantinian era" is a datum of modern history that undergirds all the fickle fluctuations of the spiritual pulse of Western (especially North American) civilization. From this point onwards, Christians who are in earnest about their faith must live in a world where *their* faith represents one alternative, and can count on no external props or head starts. Being a Christian today and tomorrow becomes a matter of decision, and the decision will have to be made over and over again, always in the context of alternatives and of "evidence to the contrary." It can no longer be assumed that generation after generation will be eased into the churches by the sheer force of social convention.

This can be regarded as a desparate or threatening situation only by those who are committed to an a priori version of the constantinian model of the church. Given the assumptions and goals of imperial Christianity, the death of Christendom must be seen as a failure of the Christian Faith. But if one tries to read the New Testament without the dubious benefits of constantinian assumptions, one may begin to believe that this "death" could be a highly provocative experience, as death so often is! This "end" could mark a new beginning, as endings so often do! As I have put it elsewhere, "The End of Christendom *could be* the beginning of the Church!" It is just conceivable at this juncture in history—precisely *because* imperial Christianity becomes an impossible way—that the alternative of that prophetic form of biblical faith which tried throughout the centuries to assert itself against Christian triumphalism might become a truly serious, normative model of the church!

The *positive* implications of this ending are thus many. But for our present deliberations there is also an instructive *negative* implication. For what the demise of constantinian arrangements means is that the imperial missionizing assumptions of historic Christianity are no longer really pertinent or even realistic. They are strictly dated assumptions. Whatever one may say about the mass baptisms of Charlemagne or the 19th century Christian blitzes on Asia and Africa, such activities were at least somehow credible in their historical contexts; for Christianity in those contexts could count on the backing of powerful empires. But when Christian denominations emerge in our own time with plans to take the earth by storm, even when they can count on plenty of *money* to back their efforts, they strain our credulity. The ways of imperial Christendom, whether Protestant or Catholic, convervative biblicist or liberal cultural, simply do not work in a religiously pluralistic world where even avowedly "Christian" regimes can no longer afford politically to assume the stance of *Defensor Fidei*. Christians who act along the lines of empire today simply do not know what time it is.

Not only is time *denying us* Christians our time-honored role as cultic saviours and heroes, but simultaneously time (providence!) is *offering us* a new role, or rather an old one that we have never quite tried out! We shall say no more about the reasons why that new/old role has become possible. Our cultural analysis in Chapter III must suffice for now. It is enough to remember that what could be entertained only by the most pessimistic observers in the past, people like Spengler who wrote of the decline of the West, is now the subject of every Hollywood movie. The formerly buoyant industrial society limps uncertainly from one news broadcast to the next. Rationality, which was supposed to have saved us all, is no longer trusted even by ordinary people. The institutions of democracy flounder and are the prey of every terrorist. No one speaks any more about Humanity, or History of Progress—all the Great Words have a hollow ring after Auschwitz. . .

And who cares?

It is hard to find anyone who *cares* in the "age of diminishing expectations" (C. Lasch). Who really cares for the forests, the land, the sea, the human beings, the animals, the future? Who cares enough for the world to rise above the pursuit of pleasure and escape and become the champion of justice, equality, international sanity, the future of the biosphere?

5 Conclusion: Stewardship as Theological Possibility and Worldly Necessity

Christians have never really cared unqualifiedly. We have admitted that already. But neither have they been quite free to say openly that they do *not* care about the earth and its creatures. They have hovered on the verge of absolute world denial, but with that Cross at the center they could hardly turn their backs altogether on the world.

What if now we cast aside our qualifications, our ambivalence, our docetism, and declared in word and deed—as a matter of Christian praxis—that "We Care"? (For that is the rôle time is offering us, quite obviously!) What if this care became, not just a sentiment, an ethic, a duty but a very way of *being*? What if, in the midst of such a society, instead of showing up as a well-known religious element going about our well-known attempt at saving the world from its moral wickedness, or winning converts, or winning arguments, or influencing the powerful, or just trying to survive(!), the church began to be perceived as a community that cares for the world as such, for *its* welfare, *its* justice, *its* peace, *its* survival? What if, in place of thinking itself the dispenser of salvation whose task it is to turn as much of "the world" into "the church" as possible, the Christian community began to act out of an avowed care for this world—care which (it declares) it has learned to have in its encounter with a God whose care for the world is infinite? And so what if this community (not alone, certainly, but in company with all persons and groups of good will) began to think and plan and act and die for the preservation and enhancement of that "beloved" world? What if a religion that had acted out of the motives of mastery for so long were to begin to act out of the motives of service—not as yet another predator on the community of humankind but as neighbor to a species that fell amongst thieves? What if stewardship became our modus operandi, our characteristic stance, our way of being in the world—not an addendum, not a means to something else, not an evangelistic come-on, but the very heart of the matter?

Is it sheer idealism to think the Church of the One who was crucified for the world incapable of such depths of caring? No, it is a matter of Christian obedience and of hope. This hope is commanded of us. The attitude of stewardship is *not* just another nice but finally impractical ideal. It is a theological possibility and a political necessity. It is also now the only way. There is no future, if we are honest, for a Christianity that tries to behave after the manner of the imperial church of the past. But there is a future for the Church of the Cross, which is prepared to be as rooted in the earth as was that Cross, that prototype and means of our solidarity with the broken world. There *is* a future for a Christian community that can be truly geocentric, that does not have an axe to grind or an ideology to guard or an ulterior motive for its services, but can simply be there for humanity and the human habitation.

For Christians who are committed to a militant form of Christian "evangelism," this will no doubt seem a retreat from faith, an escape into Christian humanism, a loss of missionary zeal. Certainly it does involve letting go of mission in the sense in which mission has been largely understood and practiced in Christendom. We could not legitimately play the part of steward and have something else besides caring as our ultimate aim—for instance the conversion of those for whom we cared. But does giving priority to stewardship as our way of being really mean the *loss* of our mission?

On the contrary, I should say that it means gaining it! The loss of a *form* of mission does not mean the loss of the Christian mission any more than the loss of a *form* of the church (even if that form is sixteen centuries old) means the loss of the church! I take it as the essence of Christian reasonableness today to think, in fact, that the only authentic form of mission in which, after such an imperial history as ours, Christianity could engage and still be *credible*, would be a form of mission that emerged out of the kind of solidarity with the earth and humankind implied in the symbol of the steward. We should not fear going in that direction, assuming that rôle. If we were able genuinely to establish our *care* in and for the world, the opportunities for us to tell about the *reason* for our care would certainly not diminish.

For real love in this world, for this world, is a rare thing! And even at its most decadent and cynical, humanity is still made curious by love. "See how these Christians *love* one another!" said some of the old pagans of Rome, waiting for the spectacles of the arena. And in a world where love is rare, and where especially *love of the world* is rare, is it not conceivable that some would remark, "See, how these Christians *love the world*!"—which would be a much better (because more biblical) remark than the one of the ancient pagans, by the way. And then would it not happen, sometimes, that this worldly curiosity would pass beyond the casual remark and become a serious question—even on occasion a question of "ultimate concern?" "Why? Why, Christians, do you strive for the welfare of this second-rate planet? Why do you seek justice for the oppressed? Why do you give up your shares in profitable multi-nationals? What do you expect to gain from your associations with these poor and powerless people? Why do you struggle against inequality and starvation and despair? Why are you expending so much psychic energy in the pursuit of peace? Why have you pitted yourselves against death? Why do you hope, Christians?"

And *then* the Christians would tell their story, judiciously, unpretentiously. *Then* they would give the reason for their hope. And sometimes their story would be smiled over, and the word "idealist" might be whispered, and the polite of the world might say that "we shall hear you again on this matter." But sometimes the story and the reason and the hope would fall on fertile ground . . .

And would this not be mission? And would it not be *authentic* mission, being the response to a question and not (as so much "evangelism" is) the answer to questions nobody asks; being grounded in praxis and solidarity and not (as so much theology is) just another petty ideology vying for the souls of humans; being attested by life and death and not (as so much religion is!) merely words and piety and rumors of miracles?

Yes, it would be mission. It would not be enormously successful. It would not conquer the world. It would not convert, baptize, confirm, marry, and bury everybody! But it would be . . . enough.

NOTES

Introduction Footnotes

[1] "Today Christianity is involved everywhere in a *double confrontation*: with the great world religions on the one hand and with the non-Christian "secular" humanisms on the other. And today the question is thrust even on the Christian who has hitherto been institutionally sheltered and ideologically immunized in the churches: compared with the world religions and modern humanisms, is Christianity something essentially different, really something special?" (Hans Küng, *On Being a Christian*, trans. by Edward Quinn (Glasgow, Wm. Collins, Sons and Co. Ltd., 1978): p. 23). One might say of the entire church in North America that it has been, until now, "institutionally sheltered and ideologically immunized." But since World War II the question Küng here identifies has become our question, too.

[2] *Haushalterschaft* is not a particularly good equivalent. As T. A. Kantonen observes, "The German word *Haushalterschaft* . . . retains too faithfully the economic connotation of the *oikonomia* of classical Greek. Various substitutes have been offered ranging from *Treuhaenderschaft*, trusteeship, to *Liebesdankbarkeit*, gratitude of love. Each of them expresses some important aspect of stewardship but not its full significance. The disposition today is to give up the search for a new word and either to endow *Haushalterschaft* with a richer meaning or simply to use the English word stewardship." (*A Theology for Christian Stewardship* (Philadelphia, The Muhlenberg Press) p.4

[3] E.g. Helge Bratgard, *Im Haushalt Gottes: Eine Theologische Studie uber Grundgedanken und Praxis der Stewardship* (Berlin, Lutherisches Verlagshaus, 1964)

[4] See Tracy Early, *Simply Sharing: A Personal Survey of How the Ecumenical Movement Shares Its Resources* (Geneva, World Council of Churches, Risk Book Series, 1980), p. 33

[5] Quoted by Kantonen, *op. cit.*, p. 1.

[6] In 1976 Anthony Storr wrote that since the end of World War II "there were only three calendar years during which [the U.S.A.] was not involved in armed conflict: 1956, 1957, and 1959. That's only three years in three decades! Since the peace of 1945 there has been an armed conflict somewhere in this world, on the average, every five months. In the first three decades of the twentieth century, Europe fought 74 wars—more than in the previous 800 years! In the nearly eight decades since the beginning of this century some 100 million people have died at the hands of their fellowmen! (*Human Aggression* (New York, Penguin Press, 1976), p. 9)

[7] Geo. S. Siudy in an article entitled, "Stewardship and Renewal in the Church," reports that one third of the 90 persons he questioned about stewardship ("What is stewardship?") expressed negative feelings: " ' . . . the word triggers in me an unbearable sense of duty and guilt. When I hear the word I want to run,' " said one of these. (*Journal of Stewardship*, Vol. 34, 1981; p. 7)

[8] I owe this discussion to W. L. Visser't Hooft, who, in a recent World Council of Churches publication says, "The word talent suggests an aptitude with which we were born. But a *charisma* is a gift which belongs to our second nature." ("The Economy of the Charismata & the Ecumenical Movement" in *Empty Hands: An Agenda for the Churches* (Geneva, W.C.C., no date provided, p. 32)).

[9] In particular, see Gustavo Gutierrez, *A Theology of Liberation*, translated by Sister Caridad Inda and John Eagleson (Maryknoll, N.Y., Orbis Books, 1973), "Theology as Critical Reflection on Praxis," pp. 6-15.

[10] Sergio Torres and John Eagleson, Eds., *Theology in the Americas*, (Maryknoll, N.Y., Orbis Books, 1976); p. 435.

There is of course a certain danger in Praxis-Theology, as in every other theological method. In this case it is that those who are intellectually lazy or constitutional 'activists' will welcome such an emphasis as a way of avoiding serious theoretical reflection. Against all such, the words of C.F. von Weizsacker are to the point: "Anyone neglecting to further his theoretical understanding of our complex world as much as he can, will in the longrun do more harm than good in his practical efforts." (*The Relevance of Science: Creation and Cosmogony* (Gifford Lectures 1959-60; London, Collins, 1964) p. 9)

[11] See my booklet, *This World Must Not Be Abandoned! Stewardship: Its Worldly Meaning* (Published by five Canadian denominations (Anglican, Lutheran, Presbyterian, Roman Catholic, and The United Church of Canada) in 1981.

Chapter I Footnotes

[1] The term is Karl Barth's, and it is one of Barth's most insightful contributions to the discussion of the nature of Christian theology. "Strictly speaking," he wrote towards the end of his life, ". . . the word 'theology' fails to exhaust the meaning of 'evangelical theology,' for one decisive dimension of the object of theology is not expressed clearly in it. This dimension is the free love of God that evokes the response of free love, his grace (*charis*) that calls for gratitude (*eucharistia*). 'Theoanthropology' would probably express better what is at stake here." (*Evangelical Theology*, translated by Grover Foley, New York, Holt, Rinehard & Winston, 1963; p. 12)

[2] "Truth, divine truth, then is not the conformity of the mind to a divine message uttered ages ago, but the discernment of present evil judged by this message and the discovery of the redemptive movement in history promised by this message. The norm of theological truth, then, is not drawn from an analogy with classical philosophy; it is drawn rather from its role in the ongoing process of world-building." (Gregory Baum, in Sergio Torres and John Eagleson, Ed., *Theology in the Americas, op. cit.*, p. 404)

[3] From the article on *Haushalter* in *Biblisch-Theologisches Handworterbuch: Zur Lutherbibel und zu neuern Ubersetzungen* (Gottingen, Vanderhoeck & Ruprecht, 1964; p. 241).

[4] The two New Testament references to stewardship to which I have not alluded in the foregoing are Titus 1:07, which insists that "a bishop, as God's steward, must be blameless," and the famous parable of the unjust steward (Luke 16)—perhaps the most difficult parable in the New Testament. One commentator believes that the thrust of this parable is against "the leaders of Israel as stewards of God's property. They should be making friends of those whom they have oppressed, so as to find security when their own present position of worldly privilege collapses with the end of the old order . . . . If they have not discharged their stewardship faithfully, including the use of their usurped privilege for the benefit of those whom they now treat as outcasts, they will not be entrusted with the riches of the King-

dom . . . which belong to Christ and his followers.' (Matthew Black, Ed., *Peake's Commentary on the Bible* (London, Thos. Nelson & Sons, 1962); p. 836.) If this interpretation is accurate, the parable has overtones similar to other passages we have mentioned, which draw attention to the *dangers* of stewardship, especially through the misuse of this 'privileged' position for purposes of personal aggrandizement. The parable can also be read in the light of the eschatological dimension treated above. I have refrained from discussing it in the body of my text, however, because it is capable of so many different interpretations, and my discussion here is necessarily circumscribed.

[5] Kantonen quips that "Since *sti* [a shorter form of *stig*] came to have the same meaning which it still retains in *sty*, it would not be amiss to render the literal meaning of steward as sty warden, keeper of swine." But, he continues in a more serious vein, "Already in Middle English . . ., it had general reference to anyone who manages the household property of another." (*A Theology for Stewardship, op. cit.* p. 3)

[6] *Cf.* Ronald D. Petry, *Partners in Creation: Stewardship for Pastor and People* (Elgin, Ill., The Brethren Press, 1980; Chapter I.)

[7] I am relying heavily here on Tillich's discussion. The six characteristics of the symbol, according to his analysis (*Dynamics of Faith*, New York, Harper Torchbooks, 1957; pp. 41 ff.) are: (1) Symbols point beyond themselves, (2) They participate in the reality they symbolize; (3) they open "levels of reality which otherwise are closed for us"; (4) they also "unlock dimensions and elements of our soul which correspond to the dimensions and elements of reality"; (5) they cannot be intentionally produced or destroyed; (6) they come to be when the situation is ripe for them. *All* these characteristics are apropos the discussion of stewardship.

Chapter II Footnotes

[1] There is, I think, a need for a *comprehensive* study of the subject. Most of the available material seems to concern itself (quite understandably in the light of the foregoing discussions) with the functional use of the metaphor. For further reading see: L.P. Powell, "Stewardship in the History of the Christian Church" (in *Stewardship in Contemporary Theology*, Ed. T.K. Thompson, N.Y., 1960); by the same author, *Money and the Church: The Story of Church Support Through the Ages—From Simony to Bingo—and What True Stewardship Means*; George A.E. Salstrand, Th. D., *The Story of Stewardship: In the United States of America* (Grand Rapids, Baker Book House, 1956).

[2] See for example Lewlie Dewart, *The Future of Belief: Theism in A World Come of Age* (London, Burns and Oates, 1966)

[3] See *The Reality of the Gospel and the Unreality of the Churches* (Philadelphia, The Westminster Press, 1975); *Has the Church A Future?* (Westminster, 1980); and the essay entitled "Mission as a Function of Stewardship", in *Spotlighting Stewardship* (W.D. Goodger, Editor: Toronto, the United Church of Canada, a CANEC publication. 1981: pp. 18-45).

[4] *op. cit.*, p. 13

[5] Salstrand, *op. cit.*, p. 31

Chapter III Footnotes

[1] Jacques Ellul, *The Technological Society* (N.Y., Alfred A. Knopf, 1964); p. 16

[2] Particularly in *Player Piano*

[3] *Op.cit.*, p. 43

[4] *Technology and Empire: Perspectives on North America* (Toronto, House of Anansi, 1969), p. 137

[5] Report of a speech given by the author on 'Literature and Technology', at the St. Laurence Centre, Toronto (*Toronto Star*, Mar. 1, 1972, p. 10)

[6] *Who Is Man?*, p. 67, Stanford, University of California Press, 1965)
[7] Emil Fackenheim, *Quest for Past and Future: Essays in Jewish Theology* (Bloomingdale and Landon, Indiana University Press, 1968); p. 232
[8] Walter M. Miller, *Canticle for Leibowitz* (Montreal, Bantam Books of Canada Ltd., 1959)
[9] *The Relevance of Science: Creation and Cosmogony* (Gifford Lectures, 1959-60; London, Collins, 1964), p. 9
[10] See the discussion of stewardship and capitalism in Chapter V.
[11] "The natural science of Darwin and Newton has shown us that nature can be understood without the idea of final purpose. In that understanding nature appears to us as indifferent to what have been considered the highest moral purposes. We can control nature but it does not sustain good." (George Grant, *Time as History*, Massey Lectures. CBC, 1969; Chapter IV)
[12] *Beyond Freedom and Dignity* (N.Y., Alfred A. Knopf, 1971)
[13] Skinner, *Freedom and the Control of Man*, p. 59
[14] April 19, 1976, p. 20
[15] E.g. Heidegger's distinction between *rechnendes Denken* and *besinnliches Denken*
[16] Heschel, *op.cit.*, p. 15
[17] *People of Paradox: An Inquiry Concerning the Origins of American Civilization* (New York and Toronto, Oxford, Univ. Press, 1972); pp. 281-82
[18] *The Culture of Narcissism: American Life in an Age of Diminishing Expectations* (N.Y.C., W.W. Norton & Co. Inc., 1978); p. 4
[19] *Fallible Man*, trans. by C. Kelbley (Chicago, Regnery, 1965); p. 223
[20] Referring to the last American election, John S. Bennett writes: "Last year's national election was not won by a large popular majority . . . almost half of those eligible failed to vote." (*The Christian Century*, Vol. XCVIII, No. 32, Oct. 14, 1981; p. 1018)
[21] Harmondsworth, Penguin Books Ltd.; first published 1940; Penguin edition 1962); p. 141

Chapter IV Footnotes

[1] "North Americans comprise about 6% of the world's population and consume approximately 40% of the world's raw materials." (*Consumer Society Notes*, Vol. 1, No. 2, December 1975; p. 2; published by the Science Council of Canada.)
[2] *Church and Colonialism*, trans. by Wm. McSweeney (Danville, N.J., Dimension Books, 1969), p. 111.
[3] Greek word for power.
[4] Dorothee Sölle writes: "Mythology and withdrawal from the world are only two sides of the same coin of hopelessness. Such hopelessness expects nothing more from man, and it triumphs today in the form of . . . [an] orthodoxy, which is not yet rid of that disdain for humanity characteristic of late antiquity and the late Middle Ages, a disdain that sees itself as devotion to God." *Political Theology*, trans. by John Shelley (Philadelphia, Fortress Press, 1971): p. 52.
[5] Jeremy Rifkin with Ted Howard, *The Emerging Order: God in the Age of Scarcity* (New York, G.P. Putnam's Sons, 1979).

Rifkin's account of 'the new evangelism,' while journalistic, is both informative and provocative theologically and historically. He characterizes (and perhaps caricatures?) the search for "an alternative Christian environment" in the following scenario: "For tens of millions of evangelical Christians, the notion of a Christian reality and an alternative Christian community is no longer just Sunday morning church rhetoric. Christians can now spend an entire day within an evangelical context, even as they continue to function in the broader secular culture.

In the morning, husband and wife wake up to an evangelical service on their local Christian owned and operated radio station. The husband leaves for work where he will start his day at a businessman's prayer breakfast. The evangelical wife bustles the children off to their Christian Day School. At mid-morning she relaxes in front of the TV set and turns on her favorite Christian soap opera. Later in the afternoon, while the Christian husband is attending a Christian business seminar, and the children are engaged in an after school, Christian sports program, the Christian wife is doing her daily shopping at a Christian store, recommended in her Christian Business Directory. In the evening the Christian family watches the Christian World News on TV and then settles down for dinner. After dinner, the children begin their Christian school assignments. A Christian baby-sitter arrives—she is part of a baby-sitter pool from the local church. After changing into their evening clothes, the Christian wife applies a touch of Christian make-up, and then they're off to a Christian nightclub for some socializing with Christian friends from the local church. They return home in the evening and catch the last half hour of the "700 Club," the evangelical Johnny Carson Show. The Christian wife ends her day reading a chapter or two from Marabel Morgan's best selling Christian book, *The Total Woman*. Meanwhile her husband leafs through a copy of *Inspiration* magazine, the evangelical *Newsweek*, before they both retire for the evening. (*Op.cit.*, pp. 125-126)

[6] *Men in Dark Times*, (N.Y. and London, Harcourt Brace Jovanovich, 1955); pp. 261-262.

[7] Especially in *Lighten Our Darkness: Towards an Indigenous Theology of the Cross* (Philadelphia, The Westminster Press, 1976)

[8] *Letters and Papers from Prison* (London, S.C.M. Press, 1971); pp. 336 f.

Chapter V Footnotes

[1] *The Canada Crisis* (Toronto, Anglican Book Centre, 1980)

[2] Fyodor Dostoevsky, *The Brothers Karamazov*, trans. by Constance Garnett (London, William Heinemann Ltd., 1912); p. 332

[3] *People of Paradox, op.cit.*, pp. 150-151

[4] "Looking Back Into the History of Ecumenical Sharing," in *Empty Hands, op.cit.*, p. 53

[5] George A.E. Salstrand, *The Story of Stewardship: In the United States of America* (Grand Rapids, Mich., Baker Book House, 1956; p. 31

[6] "Nothing in Calvinism *per se* led automatically to capitalism. But in a society already becoming capitalistic, Reformed Protestantism reinforced the triumph of new values. Puritanism undermined obstacles which the more rigid customs of Catholicism had imposed." (Michael Kammer, *op.cit.*, p. 155).

[7] *Op.cit.*, p. 6.

[8] D. B. Robertson, Ed., *Love and Justice: Selections from the Shorter Writings of Reinhold Niebuhr* (Cleveland & N.Y., Meridian Books, World Publishing Co., 1967); p. 89 f.

[9] *Stewardship in the New Testament Church: A Study in the Teachings of Saint Paul Concerning Christian Stewardship* (Richmond, John Knox Press)

[10] p. 143

[11] pp. 146-147

[12] *Ibid.*, p. 147

[13] Michael Crichton, *The Great Train Robbery* (Bantam Books, 1976); p. xiii

[14] *Political Theology*, trans. by John Shelley (Philadelphia, The Fortress Press, 1971); p. 47

Chapter VI Footnotes

[1] "The Liberation of the Middle Class," in *Journal of Stewardship*, Vol. 34, 1981; pp. 51-52.

[2] *Experiences of God* (Philadelphia, The Fortress Press, 1980); p. 26

[3] Senator M. Lamontagne, "A Science Policy for Canada," in *Consumer Notes*, Vol. 1, No. 2, Dec., 1975; published by The Science Council of Canada.

[4] Donald Thompson, *Conserver Society Notes*, Vol. 1, No. 2, Dec, 1975; p. 17 (*N.B.*: Non-Canadian readers should realize that Canadians, unlike most Americans, enjoy government-sponsored Medicare coverage; so that government spending in the area of medicine is *not* a minor item!)

[5] In the city of Saskatoon, Saskatchewan, I was a member of the lay board of a Community Health Clinic (one of several in that Province). The clinic and its very up-to-date equipment was owned by its membership; the doctors were paid very adequate salaries; the medical care I received then was better and more personal than ever before or since.

In this clinic a prescription service was instituted during my tenure as board member. All the (approx. 20) doctors agreed to prescribe the same brands (chosen from a variety). A small drug outlet was established on the premises, and in spite of this cost *plus* the cost of employing pharmacists and assistants it was possible to sell members of the clinic their prescriptions *and* certain patent medicines (like aspirins, etc.) at vastly reduced costs.

[6] Stuart J. Kingma, "Mere Survival or a More Abundant Life?" in *The Ecumenical Review* (Vol. 33, No. 3, July 1982); pp. 259-60

[7] Harry Ferguson, UPI, *Oakland Tribune*, Dec. 14, 1965 (Quoted in *The Dynamics of Change*, by Don Fabun (Englewood Cliffs, N.J., Prentice-Hall, Inc., 1968); p. 27)

[8] *The Denial of Death*, by Ernest Becker (N.Y., The Free Press, 1973); p. 187

[9] All taken from Kingma, *op.cit.*, p. 259

[10] E. F. Schumacher, *Small Is Beautiful: Economics as if People Mattered* (N.Y., Harper and Row, Publishers, 1975); p. 168

[11] Kingma, *op.cit.*

[12] *Ecology and the Politics of Scarcity* (San Francisco, W.H. Freeman and Co., 1977); p. 207

[13] Schumacher, *op.cit.*, pp. 167-168

[14] There may, as some argue, be sufficient resources for all earth's peoples—and for even more than the present world population; but not, certainly, if *all* expect to live at our speed!

[15] *Op.cit.*, pp. 169-170

[16] *Ibid.*, p. 168

[17] p. 197

[18] A gift of knowledge is infinitely preferable to a gift of material things. There are many reasons for this. Nothing becomes 'one's own' except on the basis of some genuine effort or sacrifice. A gift of material goods can be appropriated by the recipient without effort or sacrifice; it therefore rarely becomes 'his own' and is all too frequently and easily treated as a mere windfall. A gift of intellectual goods, a gift of knowledge, is a very different matter. Without a genuine effort of appropriation on the part of the recipient there is no gift. To appropriate the gift and make it one's own is the same thing, and 'neither moth nor rust doth corrupt.' The gift of material goods makes people dependent, but the gift of knowledge makes them free—if it is the right kind of knowledge, of course. (*Ibid.*, p. 197)

Chapter VII Footnotes

[1] *Science*, Vol. 155, Mar. 10, 1967: pp. 27 ff.

[2] Vol. 24, July, 1980; p. 27

[3] *Op.cit.*, p. 27 ff.

[4] *Silent Spring* (Connecticut, Fawcett Publications Inc., 1967); p. 12

[5] Quoted by Basil Willey, *The Seventeenth Century Background* (Garden City, N.Y., Doubleday Anchor Book, 1953); pp. 95-96

[6] *Discourse on Method*, trans. by Laurence J. Lafleur (The Liberal Arts Press, 1950) p. 40.

[7] From Russell's *Scientific Outlook* (p. 151), quoted by Reinhold Niebuhr in *Faith and History: A Comparison of Christian and Modern Views of History* (N.Y., Charles Scribner's Sons, 1951; p. 87)

[8] George P. Grant, *Philosophy in the Mass Age* (Toronto, The Copp Clark Publishing Co., 1959); p. vi

[9] From *Moneysworth*, Nov. 26, 1973 (reproduced in *Conserver Society Notes,* Vol. 1, No. 2, Dec. 1975; published by the Science Council of Canada, p. 15.)

[10] (New York, Alfred A. Knopf, 1977); p. 30

[11] One of the most important distinctions between the Reformed and the Luthern sides of the Reformation was that Luther retained this mystic sense in a way that neither Calvin nor Zwingli did. It informs for example his doctrine of the Lord's Supper. For the Reformers influenced by the Humanist tradition (Calvin and Luther as well as Melanchthon) bread was bread! It might symbolize or signify something else, but it remained bread. For Luther the bread, *because* it is natural, can be the vehicle of divine grace and mystery: *finitum capax infiniti.* Luther was opposed to 'natural theology'; but he never lost his sense of the "depth" of nature. North American Christianity was unfortunately not deeply touched by Lutheranism; it was the Reformed side that triumphed here.

[12] J.S. Whale, *Christian Doctrine*

[13] The distinction I am making here is between an ontological (or subsantialist) and a relational understanding of *imago Dei.* I believe that the former belongs to the Greek and Hellenistic influence upon Christianity. The Bible thinks relationally.

[14] *Op.cit.,* p. 27

[15] "God *is* love"

[16] *Cf. Silence,* trans. by William Johnston (Rutland, Vermont & Tokyo, Sophia University, 1969). (I have written an article on this work, entitled "Rethinking Christ: Theological Reflections on Shusaku Endo's *Silence,*" in *Interpretation,* Vol. XXXIII, No. 3, July, 1979.)

[17] Moltmann, *Experiences of God, op.cit.,* p. 59

[18] William Ophuls, *op.cit.,* pp. 242-243

[19] *The Pocket History of American Painting* (N.Y., Washington Square Press Inc., 1962); p. 34

Chapter VIII Footnotes

[1] I am of course speaking here to one side of the necessity for dialogue only. The other side is the need that comes from inside the Christian community itself. It *must* have dialogue with the world in order to discover the appropriate expressions of its message within its given context. Today it is no longer possible for the *koinonia* to rely upon one discipline for this dialogue (philosophy was the traditional dialogue-partner of theology). Even to do its own 'proper work' in the world (i.e. to engage in its Mission), the church today must have interdisciplinary dialogue. (I have discussed this in an article entitled, "Who Tells The World's Story?" in *Interpretation* (Vol. XXXVI, No. 1, Jan. 1982; pp. 47 ff)

[2] *Newsweek Magazine.* Nov. 23, 1981, "Anti-Nukes, U.S. Style", p. 40

[3] *The Churchman,* Vol. CXC, No. 7, October 1976; p. 9

[4] Karl Jaspers, *The Future of Mankind* (Chicago and London, The University of Chicago Press, 1961); p. 4

[5] United Church of Canada, *Issue* No. 24, December, 1980; p. 5

[6] From a section entitled, "Stewardship and Disarmament" in J. Rifkin, *The Emerging Order, op.cit.,* pp. 267-268

[7] I am indebted to my colleague, Principal Pierre Goldberger, for this insight.

[8] Supra, pp. 117-118

[9] Dorothee Sölle, *Political Theology, op.cit.,* p. 91

[10] By West German poet. Erich Fried (Whoever wants the world/to stay as it is/doesn't really want the world/to stay)

[11] *Men in Dark Times, op.cit.,* pp. 4-5

Chapter IX Footnotes

[1] *The Emerging Order, op.cit.,* pp. 270-271